NEW FAIRFIELD FREE PUBLIC LIBRARY

3 9297 00120948 2

W9-BOO-281

Home Renovation Checklist

NEW FAIRFIELD FREE PUBLIC
LIBRARY
NEW FAIRFIELD, CT.

Other McGraw-Hill Books by Robert Irwin

Home Renovation Checklist

Robert Irwin

McGraw-Hill

New York   Chicago   San Francisco   Lisbon   London   Madrid   Mexico City
Milan   New Delhi   San Juan   Seoul   Singapore   Sydney   Toronto

The McGraw·Hill Companies

Copyright © 2003 by McGraw Hill. All rights reserved. Printed in the United States of America. Except as permitted under the United States Copyright Act of 1976, no part of this publication may be reproduced or distributed in any form or by any means, or stored in a data base or retrieval system, without the prior written permission of the publisher.

1 2 3 4 5 6 7 8 9 0   DOC/DOC   0 9 8 7 6 5 4 3

ISBN 0-07-141503-3

McGraw-Hill books are available at special quantity discounts to use as premiums and sales promotions, or for use in corporate training programs. For more information, please write to the Director of Special Sales, Professional Publishing, McGraw-Hill, Two Penn Plaza, New York, NY 10121-2298. Or contact your local bookstore.

This book contains the author's opinions. Neither the publisher nor the author make representations or warranties with respect to the accuracy or completeness of the contents of this book. They specifically disclaim any implied warranties of fitness or merchantability for a particular purpose. The strategies and advice suggested in this book may not be suitable for your situation. Neither the author nor the publisher are engaged in rendering investment, legal, tax, architectural, construction or other professional services. If these services are required, you should obtain them from a professional.

 This book is printed on recycled, acid-free paper containing a minimum of 50% recycled, de-inked fiber.

Library of Congress Cataloging-in-Publication Data

Irwin, Robert, 1941–
    Home renovation checklist / Robert Irwin.
        p.   cm.
    ISBN 0-07-141503-3 (alk. paper)
    1. Dwellings—Remodeling.   2. Contractors—Selection and appointment.   I. Title.
    TH4816.I75   2003
    643'.7—dc21

                                        2003002233

Contents

Introduction

Are you considering doing a home renovation, big or small? Are you wondering what you can do yourself? What you should have the contractor do? Are you concerned about the contract you'll sign? Are you troubled by the possibility of finding lead, asbestos, or black mold when demolition begins? Do you wonder about building permits and blueprints?

Much of successfully renovating your home is simply keeping track of what you need to do and knowing how to handle problems that crop up. If you don't know, you won't plan for it. And if you don't plan for it, it can cost you big bucks when it suddenly rears up.

Wouldn't it be nice if there were a home renovation checklist of all the things you should keep track of, plan for, and take care of? Wouldn't it be great to have this checklist *before* you began the work? Wouldn't it be terrific to have it handy to answer questions *while* work progresses? Wouldn't it be comforting to know that someone else had been through this before, was anticipating your problems, and was providing solutions?

That's what this book offers you. It's a checklist of the things you should ask yourself, your contractor, your architect, and your lawyer when you tackle a renovation project for the first time or the tenth time. It instantly converts you from someone who doesn't know or isn't sure, to a savvy renovator who really does know it all.

Check the lists in this book (along with their explanations), and you'll avoid those horrible pitfalls that "the other guy or gal" plummets into.

How to Use This Book

Take it with you when you talk to a contractor or are fill-
ing out a contract. Refer to it when you're checking out
kitchen appliances in a store, when you're ordering
plumbing fixtures from a building supply house, or when
you're trying to decide what to renovate in your kitchen,
bath, or bedroom.

Keep this book handy when you decide to install flooring or lights, countertops or cabinets, faucets or toilets.
Are you unsure about how to go about handling electrical
work? Check out the pages in this book. This is your
guide, your checklist to getting the job done right, the
first time, at a budget price.

Keep in mind that for every question in this book,
there's also an explanation. You're not left out in the cold
wondering what you should do. You're given the information to come up with a solution to your problem. Once
you check the question *and* the answer, you know you've
covered the topic. Let this book show you how it feels to
be the expert at home renovation.

1
Hiring the Contractor

Questions to Ask Yourself

Have I sought a recommendation? ☐ yes ☐ no

Since 2000, the pace of renovation work in this country has been the heaviest in history. In almost all neighborhoods people are remodeling their homes. If your immediate neighbors haven't, chances are they know of someone nearby who has. Contact that neighbor. You'll usually get the double benefit of a contractor recommendation, plus a chance to look at the work that contractor actually did in a home similar to yours. Also drive around your neighborhood and look for signs that contractors post in yards where they are working. And ask around in your circle of friends and with associates at work. There's nothing quite as good as a personal recommendation from someone who has actually used a contractor and liked the work.

Have I checked out contractor websites? ☐ yes ☐ no

In the old days the yellow pages of the phone book were the bottom line for finding a contractor. Today it's the web. Use a search engine and key words such as "building contractor," and be sure to put in your location. (Keep in mind, that the web is worldwide—you don't want a contractor from Pittsburgh if you live in Phoenix!) Many contractors will not only list their services, but will also provide images of work they have done. In addition to finding someone local, be sure to look for a contractor who specializes in the type of work you want done—windows and doors, kitchens, additions, and so on.

Do I know someone in the buildings trades?   ☐ **yes** ☐ **no**

You may know a plumber, a carpenter, an electrician, or someone else who works in construction. Be sure to talk with these people and ask them who's good at renovation work. As with all fields, insiders will know the good apples from the bad. They can quickly tell you whom to avoid and can recommend those to use. And often they can give you solid reasons for their opinions. Sometimes you'll have to use a "friend of a friend" to get the recommendations you need. Just keep working your way through until you have the solid information you need.

Have I considered contractors who "stop by?"   ☐ **yes** ☐ **no**

These days, contractors or their reps will often stop door-to-door and ask if you have considered doing any renovation work, and if so, if you will let them give you an estimate. There's nothing wrong with this. However, be sure to ask them how they happened to find you. If they're doing work on a neighborhood home, ask to see it. Be wary of renovators who canvas whole cities and then move on. Sometimes they're in for "quick and dirty" work; their bids are high and their work questionable. Read on for further suggestions about things you should ask them.

Have I checked with my state's contractor licensing board?   ☐ **yes** ☐ **no**

All contractors should be licensed. Usually states limit the cost of a job that can legitimately be done by an unlicensed contractor. For example, in California an unlicensed "handyman" can only do work up to $500 in value. Each state maintains a licensing board. With the name or the license number, you should be able to call or check a website to see if your contractor has a license in good standing. You should also be able to see if there have been any complaints and actions taken against the contractor. Keep in mind that some states don't keep these records up-to-date, so you can't entirely rely on them. Check with "yourstate.gov." and search for "contractor's licensing board."

Have I checked that the contractor's license matches a driver's license?

☐ yes ☐ no

A contractor's license is typically a credit-card-sized piece of paper. It will indicate what the contractor is licensed for. (There are over 40 specialties!) Be sure that the person showing you the license is indeed the person listed there. Ask to see a driver's license and compare the two. Yes, it might be a bit awkward, but not as awkward as hiring a crook to do your work.

Have I asked the contractor for a free estimate?

☐ yes ☐ no

As soon as you have a contractor you're interested in, ask him or her to give you an estimate. This should always be free. Simply don't use a contractor who asks to be paid to bid on a job. The estimate can be given two ways. One is a ballpark figure. You discuss in general terms what you want done, and the contractor says it will cost around "X" number of dollars, but tells you not to hold him to that figure. The other kind of estimate is when you have detailed plans and a list of materials, and the contractor gives you a written bid, which you can and should hold him or her to.

Is a handshake enough?

☐ yes ☐ no

Legal books will tell you never to do business this way. However, in the construction field it's sometimes an okay way to work, *if* you know with whom you're dealing and it's a small job. For small jobs with a reputable contractor, it can be enough. If a plumber says he'll put in a sink for $250 and you shake on it, if you know the person to be reputable, it may be enough. For larger deals, shake hands, but also get a detailed written and signed bid, just to be sure that someone's memory doesn't fail later on. A good contractor will almost always want it in writing, just to be sure that he or she has documentation in order to haul you into court in case you don't pay.

Have I asked the contractor to supply references?

☐ yes ☐ no

If you haven't already seen work done by a specific contractor, ask for references; three to five is normal. Many contractors will bring out a book of pictures showing you various jobs they have done. That's fine. Just ask for the names, addresses, and phone numbers of the people whose work is shown, and ask if you can contact them. Usually, contractors will give you their most recent jobs—people who they haven't bothered as references too many times already. If a contractor can't supply references, or asks you not to call and bother the people, suspect that something is wrong. Good workmen are proud of the jobs they do, and the people who do good work are usually eager to show it off.

Have I checked out the contractor's references?   ☐ yes   ☐ no

Most people who ask for references never check them out. Don't be like this. Call. Tell the person that the contractor gave you his or her name, and ask the person if they can give a recommendation. Most people will readily tell you how happy, or disappointed, they are with the job. Then ask if you can come down and see the work. This is crucial. If you don't see it, how do you know you weren't simply talking to the contractor's brother-in-law who gets 10 bucks for every recommendation? Go and look. It will be worth your time. Besides, you may get new ideas for your own renovation in the process.

Have I called materials suppliers and lenders and asked about the contractor?   ☐ yes   ☐ no

Ask the contractor to supply you with names, addresses, and phone numbers of suppliers and lenders. Then call them. You'll quickly find out if the contractor pays his or her bills on time, has good (or bad) credit, and is held in respect (or disrepute) by these people.

Will the contractor quickly come out and look over the job?   ☐ yes   ☐ no

These days, contractors everywhere are busy. Sometimes they take on too much work. One indication of this is when a contractor doesn't have time to come right out and look at your job. If the contractor says he or she will "try to work you in" sometime in the next month, look for another contractor. This contractor simply doesn't have time to work for you. The worst thing you could do is to keep pestering until he or she does finally come out and give you a bid. If you accept it, chances are you'll have the same problems getting this contractor to come out do the work as you had getting them to bid. The job will take forever, and the delays will drive you crazy.

Will the contractor supply a set of plans?

☐ yes ☐ no

No plans are usually needed if the job is small. Having the contractor retile the counter tops with standard white tile does not usually require a set of plans. It does, however, require that you agree on exactly which tile to be used, as well as the other necessities of an agreement, as noted in the next chapter. However, if you're having a specific tile design put in, then a layout or design plan should be used. And the contractor, or you, must supply it. Many contractors, especially for small jobs, will provide you with sketches (or more detailed plans) to show you what they are planning to do. For big jobs you'll need detailed plans, sometimes from an engineer/architect.

Will the contractor submit a written bid?

☐ yes ☐ no

As noted, for anything more than a simple installation, this is a necessity. Try to get the written bid to be as detailed as possible. It should include all the work that is to be done as well as a list of specific materials to be used. Many contractors will want you to sign this bid, and in doing so, it then becomes part of a contract. However, especially if it's a big job, you probably will want a more detailed contract. Check into the next chapter to see the many requirements a good contract should have.

Should I get more than one bid?

☐ yes ☐ no

Absolutely! Some contractors will try to sweet talk you into believing that their bids are all inclusive, that is, their bids are what any other contractor would bid, so why bother looking elsewhere. Don't believe it! You will be astonished at not only the price differences usually found between bids, but the methods that different contractors will use to get the job done, as well as the different materials they may want to use. Get at minimum three separate and independent bids. Five are better. And don't get hustled into quickly accepting one because the contractor says if you don't sign right away, the price may change, or he or she won't be able to fit you in until next year. Prices remain surprisingly constant over the short term, and often it's better to wait until next year to get the right job done correctly.

Are the bids really accurate?   ☐ yes   ☐ no

Not really, at least when it comes to renovation work. The reason is that no contractor can know in advance what's going to be involved until he or she has torn out the existing work. And that's long after the bid was made. The old joke in the field is that you take the low bid, the high bid, and the in-between bid and add them all together, and that's what it's going to cost! Perhaps not quite, but keep in mind that when you're renovating, things always seem to cost more than you anticipated, and more than the contractor bid.

Have I created a spec sheet?   ☐ yes   ☐ no

Many first-time home renovators either forget about or never knew about this. A specifications sheet details exactly the materials you want. If you're going to have a faucet installed, is it a Moen or a Price-Pfister or some other brand. What is the exact model number? What is the price, and where can it be purchased for that price? Are there any delivery problems (does it need to be picked up, will it take a few weeks to get it in stock, does it need to be ordered directly from the manufacturer, etc.)? All of this information will enter into the bid that a contractor makes. If you don't have an accurate and up-to-date spec sheet, don't expect an accurate bid.

Can I save money buying my own materials?   ☐ yes   ☐ no

Many people feel that they can save money by buying their own materials. This is not usually the case because contractors typically get deep discounts from suppliers. The key is to get the contractor to pass those savings on to you. If you know your costs, ask the contractor if he or she can do better. Often they will, in order to get the job. Also, there's the matter of returns if something doesn't fit or getting a new piece if something extra is needed. If the contractor is supplying materials, he or she will have to get in the truck and pick it up. If you're supplying materials, it's going to be up to you to do that. Do you have time to leave your job or whatever else you're doing in the middle of the day to run down and get a copper elbow or three extra two-by-fours? If you don't, the contractor's crew may sit waiting until you do, and that's going to cost more money than if you had the contractor be responsible for materials.

Do I have a drawing of what I want done?   ☐ yes   ☐ no

In addition to the plan, it's also a good idea to have a realistic drawing of how you want the final work to look. If you're putting in a bathroom, what will the cabinets, counters, fixtures, lights, and so on look like? You can do the rendering yourself as a pencil sketch. Programs such as Sierra Home Architect or 3D Home Architect-Broderbund will let you create more realistic drawings, although the learning curve tends to be steep. Many materials suppliers (such as Home Depot) will create a 3-D plan showing what you intend to do, for $50 or so, which usually can be applied to the purchase of materials. Don't underestimate the value of this drawing. It will help you decide not only what you want done, but also whether it's worthwhile to do the project.

Do I need a completion bond?   ☐ yes   ☐ no

Again, it depends on the size of the job and the reputation of the contractor. A completion bond pays to complete the project if the contractor is unable to do so. It has many caveats, so it's not all-inclusive. And it's expensive, typically around five percent of the contract price. It requires the contractor to have an almost impeccable reputation, so many won't be able to qualify for it. Some lawyers recommend a completion bond on all jobs. I personally prefer not to use one. As far as I'm concerned, if the contractor can qualify for the bond, that's almost as good as getting it. On small jobs, the hassle is usually not worth it. On big jobs, such as a whole house renovation, you may want to consider it, particularly if you're concerned about the contractor's ability to perform. But then again, if you're that concerned, why use this contractor?

Have I seen the contractor's liability insurance policy?

☐ yes   ☐ no

All contractors should carry liability insurance. This is to protect both you and them in case something catastrophic should happen on the job. For example, you're putting in a new wing and in order to clear the ground a tree must be removed. In the process of removing it, it falls on your neighbor's home and someone is injured. Yes, your homeowner's may cover it. But you want your contractor to have liability insurance that will immediately step in and take care of the financial aspect of the problem. It's not enough that the contractor claims to have liability insurance. You need actually to see the policy and see that it's in force. It should be for several million dollars at minimum.

Have I seen the contractor's worker's comp policy?

☐ yes   ☐ no

All contractors should carry worker's comp. This provides medical and other coverage if a workperson should be hurt on the job. Someone is hammering in a two-by-four and hits her thumb instead of the nail. That can be an immediate trip to the hospital, not to mention time off from work. Worker's comp may pick up the cost. As with liability insurance, it's not enough that the contractor claims to have worker's comp. You need actually to see the policy and see that it's in force. Worker's comp claims have been climbing, and the cost of the policies have gone through the roof. To save money, a few contractors have let their policies lapse. That's why you need to see that the policy a contractor has will be in force during the entire construction period.

How much money should I pay the contractor up front?

☐ yes   ☐ no

This depends on the size of the job and the state you are in. Some states restrict up-front charges. In California, for example, a contractor cannot legally ask for more than 10 percent up front. The remainder should be paid as the work is completed. Sometimes, of course, the whole payment is due at the end. For example, if you were having someone install your kitchen appliances, you would normally pay for the appliances, and then, after the work was done, pay for the labor. Similarly, if someone were grading your yard, you'd normally pay after all the work was completed. For big jobs, it's normal to pay in increments. Typically, 10 percent is paid to start, and then a percentage is paid as the work progresses, with perhaps a 10-percent holdback at the end until the work is completed and approved by the local building department.

Am I being asked to pay for materials up front?   ☐ yes   ☐ no

Keep in mind that contractors usually get 30 to 45 days to pay for materials. Therefore, they don't need to get any money up front for those materials. Be wary of a contractor who wants to be paid up front for materials, particularly if those materials haven't yet been delivered. The contractor may simply not have the capital to stay in business and may be planning on living on the funds you advance.

Questions to Ask Your Contractor

How long have you been renovating homes?   ☐ yes   ☐ no

As in most things in life, experience counts. You don't want your contractor to be learning on you. You want the benefit of his or her experience in planning and completing the job. At a minimum, your contractor should have five years' experience in renovation. (Experience in new construction doesn't count as much because so much of renovation involves ripping out old work and encountering the unexpected.) Sometimes a person new to the field will give you a low bid because of his or her lack of experience. You'll have to decide whether the bid is low enough to take on the risk of inexperience. Just remember, if the contractor can't do the job as promised, you might have to go out there and hire somebody else to do it. And that could cost more than twice as much.

Can you supply local references?   ☐ yes   ☐ no

All reputable contractors can supply references. You want
a minimum of five (and remember to call them and go out
to see the work that was done). Sometimes a contractor
will say that he or she is new to the area and all the references are from a distant city. That's okay, except that it
makes it inconvenient for you. If you're interested in this
contractor, then you still have to do your due diligence—
you still have to call the distant references and go out and
see them. Some contractors will provide references, but
say that the people have requested that you not call them.
That's as good as nothing at all. A reference you can't
check doesn't help you. You want recent jobs that the contractor has done and people who are willing to praise and
show you the work.

Will you actually do or supervise the job yourself?   ☐ yes   ☐ no

Some large contractors use salespeople to sell jobs. These
are usually nothing more than building mills, and in
using them you lose a lot of your ability to judge the quality of the person involved. If the man or woman you're
dealing with isn't the one who's actually going to do the
work, or at least directly supervise it, then judging how
well they respond to your questions is almost valueless.
Remember, renovation is a personal business—not a factory job. You should meet and know the actual people
involved. After all, you'll make all sorts of requests, and
the contractor will make all sorts of commitments. You
don't want all of this lost to a middleman. Also, be wary
of salespeople who come in and show you how big and
impressive their companies are, with jobs going across
the state if not the country. You should not be impressed
by a big head office or lots of employees. They just repre-
sent money spent other than on your own job.

Are you licensed?   ☐ yes   ☐ no

It should almost go without saying, but the fact is that
many people who come representing themselves as contractors, are in fact nothing more than handymen. They
are not licensed by the state. Keep in mind that licensing

does not guarantee that you'll get a good job. It only says that the person has met some minimum requirements and should know what he or she is doing. On the other hand, for small jobs sometimes a handyman is perfect. Also, in many states a handyman cannot sue you for nonpayment of a job that normally requires a contractor's license. This is not to say that you shouldn't pay what you've agreed to. Rather, it's that the handyman, because of his or her reduced position, will often work for less and will be more willing to bend to your wishes. On the other hand, the end result may also be less then you hoped for.

Do you have worker's compensation?

☐ yes ☐ no

As I suggested earlier, this is something you ask yourself. Now, to find out, you need to ask the contractor. All contractors should carry worker's comp. And remember, you should ask to see the actual policy—ensuring that it will be in force during all of your work.

Can you be bonded?

☐ yes ☐ no

The minute you ask this question, you're likely to see the contractor turn a sour face. Many very good contractors have had bad experiences with owners and bonding companies. It's cost them time, money, and headache. And as far as they are concerned, if you want a bond, you can look for another contractor. Don't be put off by this attitude, as the bonding process is tedious and not always rewarding in the way we expect. As I said earlier, it may be enough that the contractor has the ability to be bonded. Also keep in mind that many contractors who are relatively new to the field (who have been in business less than 5 years), may have trouble qualifying for a bond or it may require a higher premium. This does not necessarily make them any less qualified or capable. Finally, if you insist on having the contractor bonded, expect to pay an additional 5 or so percent in costs.

Will you give me a total cost bid?

☐ yes ☐ no

This is especially important in renovation work. The problem is that very often, until the existing structure is ripped out, the contractor can't tell exactly how much new work will be required. Thus, inexperienced contractors will want only to give you a time and materials bid. In other words, you'll pay them so much an hour, plus materials, until the job is done. A total cost bid, on the other hand, limits the amount you must pay. Only a very experienced contractor will be able to give you this kind of bid, because if the contractor guesses wrong and it costs more, he or she will have to eat the extra. Sometimes a total cost bid can be higher simply because the contractor is padding it to handle unanticipated costs. Remember to compare bids closely from different contractors.

Will you give me a "time and materials" bid?   ☐ yes   ☐ no

As noted above, a less experienced contractor is likely to opt for this. On the other hand, if you know and trust the contractor, it may be the fairest way to go for all concerned. I've worked on a time and materials basis with contractors who were scrupulous in not overcharging. Indeed, in some cases they actually undercharged, just to be sure they were dealing fairly with me. On the other hand, once you've agreed to this, there's little to keep a contractor from hiring extra help and spending extra dollars on materials. It's kind of like the cost-plus projects that the government undertakes in the aerospace program. Of course, if you don't have the funds of Lockheed-Martin, you may want to reconsider a time and materials bid.

Can you give me a start date?   ☐ yes   ☐ no

Many contractors simply don't want to put this down in writing. They don't want you to hold them to it. Typically, they are working on a half dozen or more jobs, and they intend to fit you in when they can. If you have a start date, it forces them to focus on your project. On the other hand, starting is not the same as continuing. The contractor may show up with lumber and a crew on the appointed date and work all day, then not come by for weeks. The start date does not guarantee that your work will be done, but it does help. Further, if your contract states that the contractor will begin and continue working on your project without significant interruption, if worst comes to worst, you might have an edge in court later on.

What will happen if you don't start on that date?

☐ yes ☐ no

Be blunt. If the contractor gives you a start date, ask what happens if he or she misses it. Remember, in the construction trade there are all sorts of unforeseen things that can occur. Rain can slow down or cancel work. A building department may not be forthcoming with a permit. Materials may not arrive as anticipated. What happens when the contractor doesn't start? Expect some hemming and hawing and then a commitment to start as soon as possible after the start date. Decide if that's good enough for you. You may want a very specific commitment, and if the contractor can't start, the deal is off. You'll find someone else who can. If you put teeth into it, you may find that suddenly all the problems with preventing starting on a particular date disappear.

Can you give me a finish date?

☐ yes ☐ no

If contractors are hesitant to give you a start date, they are downright determined not to give you a finish date, and with good reason. They can't know what will happen, especially on a renovation. They could break into a wall only to discover that electricity and plumbing have to be rerouted. It could take them a week to get a plumber and an electrician out. Suddenly they're a week behind. Rip out another wall and dry rot is discovered, meaning that new ceiling beams and floor joists must be installed. A modification or rewrite of the permit may be necessary, along with building department delays, not to mention the time consumed in the unexpected work. It's simply very hard to call the day that the job will be finished. Nevertheless, you need a day to aim toward, or else the job can drag on forever. If a contractor doesn't want to put a finish date in, I ask him or her to name a date they are sure the job can be done, even if it's next year. Usually they will come up with something. Then I suggest that it's a long time till then. I ask the contractor if he or she can't reasonably expect to be done a few weeks or even a month earlier, and we work backward until the contractor reaches a point where he or she won't budge. If I can live with that date, it's done.

What will happen if you don't finish on that date?   ☐ yes   ☐ no

Having a finish date is of no great consequence, unless
there's some penalty involved in not finishing by that
date. Of course, there's always the possibility of your taking the contractor to court if the job is not completed on
time. However, in court the contractor can argue extenu-
ating circumstances (weather, illness, your changing the
plans, and so on) and often judges will agree. Therefore,
on big jobs there's often a money penalty. The contractor
will lose so much a day for each day the job is not finished
by the deadline. On most small home renovations, contractors won't work like that. The jobs are too small for
them to risk such a financial penalty. Thus, you may want
to work the other way. Offer a bonus. If the job is done
early (say a month or a week or whatever), you'll pay a
set amount of extra money. If the contract is completed on
time, you'll pay half that amount. If it's late, the contractor loses the entire bonus. The bonus doesn't have to be
large, a few thousand will do, but it's something that the
contractor will be thinking about as easy money, and will
work to get.

**Do you have a phone number I can reach you
at anytime?**   ☐ yes   ☐ no

This question is not as simple minded as it seems. Many
contractors are hard to reach. They haven't shown up and
you want to know why. Or there's a dispute between you
and the workpeople, and you need the contractor *now* to
settle it. Or you want to change the plans, and you want to
discuss it with the contractor before work continues. You
need to be confident that you can reach the contractor.
These days, most, but not all, contractors carry cell phones
with them. Be sure you get that number. And let them
know that if they change the number, you want to know
the new one. If a contractor simply says that he or she will
always be around, forget that person. Of one thing you
can be certain, a contractor will never "always" be around.

Can I buy the building supplies myself?   ☐ yes   ☐ no

Some contractors will allow you to do this. Others will
not. See an earlier question as well as the one that follows

on this topic, to see why it may be to your disadvantage to buy materials yourself. Often, owners will want to buy materials to control the cost and the money flow better. If that's the case, then consider this compromise. Set up an account in your name at a local building materials supplier. Then let the contractor charge on your account up to a specified amount. If the contractor wants to charge more, then there's a call made to you and you have to approve it. No, it's not as much control as buying things yourself. But it may be better than simply letting the contractor buy whatever and wherever he or she wants.

If I supply materials, what happens if they are defective, or break, don't fit, or you need extras?

☐ yes ☐ no

If you're determined to supply materials yourself, then you and the contractor should have a plan when things don't work out. Unless the job is very simple, like putting up shutters for example, expect the unexpected. This is doubly true when electricity and plumbing are involved. Who is going to run to the store for new supplies? Who will pay for them? If the contractor is expected to handle the problem, be sure that he or she knows about this and agrees to it. If you're expected to handle the problem, be sure that you're going to be available when needed. As noted earlier, if you have another job or other commitments, you're better off not supplying materials yourself.

How much money do you want up front?

☐ yes ☐ no

Money is what binds the deal together, so it's better to get out up front just how much is involved. As noted above, some contractors will want money to get started, while others will want their money only upon completion. Find out what your contractor prefers (or demands). Keep in mind that this is negotiable. The contractor does not want to hear that you can't afford to pay him or her. That almost certainly will nix the job. On the other hand, if you say you're uncomfortable paying 40 percent up front because no work has been done, but instead would be willing to pay 10 percent, you can probably work it out amicably. Most contractors are reasonable people—they have to be, in order to deal with owners, workers, architects, inspectors, and the host of others they come in contact with. Give them something reasonable to chew on, and usually they'll respond favorably.

Will you accept payments from a construction loan?   ☐ yes   ☐ no

Many people (about half) get financing to handle their home renovations. This may be in the form of a home equity loan. Or it could be in the form of a home improvement/construction loan. These types of loans pay the money out in increments, and only *after* certain work is completed. Thus, the contractor must, for example, finish framing the new addition before a payment will be made. And the next payment may not be made until the outside sheathing, insulation, dry walling, and rough plumbing and electrical are in. That can be a long spell for the contractor to go without a payment. It means that he or she has to have the capital to continue to pay the crew and the materials suppliers. Be sure that the contractor will agree to work this way. Be sure the contractor knows in advance when payments will be forthcoming. Be sure you've arranged financing well in advance! (See Chapter 4.)

Will you allow me to do some of the work myself?   ☐ yes   ☐ no

Ask this and you can expect some sniggers in response. You do some of the work? You're a "civilian." You're out of the picture. We're professionals. "Yes, yes," you may say. You may argue that you've had carpentry, or electrical, or whatever experience. And you can save a bundle doing it yourself. On one remodel, I did all the plumbing. Yes, I had to endure the sniggers. But when the plumbing was done, I got a few pats on the back, too. If you are truly qualified to do work yourself, then make sure that your contractor will let you do it. Some simply won't allow it, saying, if nothing else, that it's a liability issue. (It's your house, so it's questionable what liability the contractor has if you do the work.) Others will go along. Better to get this out up front than find surprises later on.

2
Checking Out the Contract

Questions to Ask Yourself

Do I need a written contract?

☐ yes ☐ no

Yes, you usually do. A written contract is the vehicle that drives the renovation work. It should tell both you and the contractor what's expected. It specifies the work to be done, the materials to be used, and the quality anticipated. It also usually specifies how much you'll pay, when, and in what form. It's normally intended as a legally binding document, so be sure that it contains everything you want it to, and uses language that you understand and that fulfills your wishes. Check into the following questions to ask both the contractor and your attorney when preparing a contract.

Do I need an attorney?

☐ yes ☐ no

You can hire someone to do work on a handshake (see Chapter 1), but you can't rely on it. If things go awry, it's going to be what you remember versus what the contractor remembers, your word against his or hers. When you have a properly written contract, it spells out exactly what was to be done, by whom, and when. It's then far easier to determine whether someone messed up. It's also wisest to have the contract checked by an attorney.

Who will supply the contract? ☐ yes   ☐ no

Normally, the contractor will have a contract that he or she will want you to sign. This, however, may not be the best contract for you. Depending on the size of the job, you may want to get your attorney involved. Regardless of the size of the job, certain "boilerplate" should be included that covers such things such as liability in case of accidental damage, providing materials to be used, how work is to be performed, and so on. Be aware that if you want to supply the contract, it will usually delay the signing. The contractor may want to run it by an attorney. And that could take more time, and potentially increase the bid.

Does the contract specify all the work to be done? ☐ yes   ☐ no

The details of a job should be as specific as possible. A description of the work to be performed will be what is looked at should there be a future disagreement, and it will also help to ensure that both you and the contractor are starting on the same page. The contract may reference certain plans or other documents. Be sure that there isn't some part of the work left out. For example, you may be hiring a contractor to excavate, grade, and pave a driveway. But you also want him or her to bring in loads of dirt for a future lawn. Be sure that all of it is covered, not just a part of it.

Does the contract specify the start date? ☐ yes   ☐ no

The contract is where the start date should go. If you have a start date but it is left out of the written contract, then it's almost like having none at all. Be sure the day, month, and year are specified. Some people feel that the start date is so important, they will insist that the contractor initial right behind the start date so he or she later can't say that they didn't notice that part of the contract. Some contracts will have it in big, bold text.

Does the contract specify the end date? ☐ yes   ☐ no

The contract is where the end date should go. As with the start date, if you have an end date, but it is left out of the written contract, then it's likely to have little effect. Be sure that it's spelled out down to the day, month, and year. It's not a bad idea to request that the contractor initial right behind the start date so the contractor later can't say that he or she didn't notice that part of the contract. Some contracts will have it in big, bold text. On the other hand, many contracts will leave it out because the contractor is unwilling to make such an important commitment. (Check the previous chapter.)

Does the contract give penalties for missing dates? ☐ yes ☐ no

Most home renovation contracts will not specify penalties for missing start or finish dates. Quite frankly, the jobs are usually too small. On the other hand, yours may be a bigger contract, or you may be more determined to have these included. If so, then they should be spelled out as clearly as possible in the contract. Since this is not a normal part of the contract, but probably will be written in, you should have your attorney do it so the language is handled correctly.

Does the contract specify who will do the work? ☐ yes ☐ no

You may think that, obviously, the contractor will be doing the work. But what if there are subcontractors to be hired? What if there are outside engineers, architects, designers, and so on who are involved? What if you are planning on doing some of the work yourself? What if you are planning on hiring some of the labor out yourself? There is an almost endless number of different ways of handling labor in a renovation. Exactly how it's to be done in your job should be carefully spelled out. By the way, it's a good idea to get the contractor's name spelled correctly and to include his or her license number.

Does the contract specify who will do (and clean up) the demolition? ☐ yes ☐ no

Usually with renovation we think only about the final product, the remodeled home. However, before we get to that there's the matter of demolishing the old and getting rid of the remains. Usually the contractor who handles the remodeling will handle demolition, but not always. For example, sometimes a specialized crew will come in to remove a roof. Or laborers may be hired to get rid of old, heavy tile. It's important to know who will supervise and otherwise be in charge. It's also important to know that the demolished parts of the old home will quickly be cleaned up and removed. A few contractors are content to work in a mess around demolished parts of walls, cabinets, and so forth. However, that's generally unsafe, may not be permitted by the city or your homeowner's association, and may be uncomfortable for you. The contract should specify who will handle cleanup, and that it should be done immediately after demolition occurs.

Does the contract specify who will handle final cleanup?   ☐ yes   ☐ no

After all of the works are completed, there is the final cleanup. This involves going inside as well as outside your home and removing any remaining usable building materials as well as any cut wood, drywall, insulation, pipe, wire, and so on that happens to be lying around. It also involves sweeping the entire work site as well as washing windows and even doors as may be necessary. Holes need to be filled, footing for foundations covered up, and in general, your place needs to be tidied. Does the contract specify that this is to be done and that the contractor is to do it?

Does the contract specify conditions to be maintained during the work?   ☐ yes   ☐ no

Most owners forget about this, but it is a critical part of any renovation. There may be a portable toilet placed on site (as required by the building department). There may be building supplies such as lumber, sheet rock, paint, and so on scattered about. There may be cut pieces of wood, nails, metal, and similar things lying around the work site. Does your contract specify that these must all be cleaned up and tidy at the end of every workday? Your homeowner's association may require this and may fine you if it's not done. If it's not in the contract, how are you going to enforce the contractor's doing it? The city may also have ordinances requiring it.

Are work hours specified?

☐ yes　☐ no

Again, most people don't think about this, but most cities have specific times during which construction is not permitted. Typically, it's after 10 at night and before 7 in the morning, but the hours may vary. These times are set out to protect your neighbors from loud noises and other nuisances created during the reconstruction process. You may have your own requirements. For example, if you sleep late and are going to be living in the house during the renovation period, you may want to specify that work does not commence before 9 or even 10 in the morning. The builder may charge extra for this inconvenience, but it may be a necessity for you. Is it all spelled out in the contract?

Is a materials spec sheet included?

☐ yes　☐ no

A builder spec sheet is a list of all the materials to be used in the renovation project. If it is attached to the contract, it becomes part of it, and later on the contractor can't argue that he or she used a Kohler sink when you specified some other brand. The list should be as detailed as possible down to manufacturer and model number. Of course, at any given time a product may not be available, and a substitution may need to be made. However, in general, the materials spec sheet keeps everyone honest. (It keeps you from claiming that you wanted a different brand of sink when the spec sheet specifically lists Kohler!) In a good spec sheet, the size and amount of lumber, even the size and type of nails to be used will be specified.

Does the contract say "job to be done in a professional, workmanlike manner"?

☐ yes　☐ no

The assumption is that when the renovation project is completed, it will look good. But how do you know? One way is to have the contract specify that all work be done to professional standards. Later on, if there's a dispute, you can point to what other professionals have done for similar projects and compare it to what your contractor did. Keep in mind that this is a gray area, and unless there is gross incompetence on the part of the contractor, it's difficult to nail down.

Does the contract give me right of approval?   ☐ yes   ☐ no

This is very important. Many owners forget to give themselves the right of approval. Without it, the builder just completes the job and demands his or her money. You could be on the hook whether you like the way it was done or not. On the other hand, if you have right of approval, then the contractor must do the work up to your standards. Most contractors will *not* want to have this included in the contract. They may feel that most owners are too wishy-washy and will waste the contractor's time and patience on endless remakes.

Does the contract specify my options if I don't approve?   ☐ yes   ☐ no

Sometimes the contractor will go along with an approval clause *if* it's linked to a specific method of remedying the problem. For example, you may have approval of only minor parts of the job. Or if the entire job is called into question, before the contractor is obligated to do any remakes, the whole matter must go before an arbitration committee made up of other contractors. Or if you disapprove, it's up to the contractor's judgment to handle the remake, and you might be billed for additional costs, if any. It's rare that a contractor will agree both to giving you approval and allowing you to dictate how remakes are to be handled.

Does the contract specify what is a change to the plans?   ☐ yes   ☐ no

You may have the best of intentions and the most solid of plans when you start your renovation. However, rest assured that half way through, your perspective will change. As you see the old walls knocked out and new areas built up, you'll realize that you want things done differently. You want to make changes. Since changes cost money, it's important for the contract to specify what constitutes a change. It is any deviation at all from the original plans? Is it a 10-percent or 20-percent difference? It's helpful for all to know how big a change you can make without it automatically triggering a price increase. Most builders will want any changes reflected in a new price.

Does the contract spell out how charges for making changes to the plans will be handled?

☐ yes   ☐ no

You'll recall earlier that I recommended you get a total price bid. However, when you start making changes, the contract may specify that the cost is now on a time and materials basis. This means that you can do anything you want, but the contractor is going to charge for every bit of it. Make a lot of changes and you can quickly double, or more, the original price! Be aware if this clause is in your contract. It's a great incentive to hold any changes to a minimum. Some contracts will specify that if changes are made, the contractor will give a new total cost bid on the changes. However, this is almost moot, since what are you going to do, switch to a new contractor half way through the job? Chances are it's easier, and in the long run, cheaper, to go along with what your current contractor charges.

Does the contract specify that the contractor has worker's comp?

☐ yes   ☐ no

As noted earlier, the contractor should carry this to protect all workers. The contract should specify that the worker's comp will remain in force during the term of the job. It should also comply with the minimum standards required by your state. As noted in the previous chapter, even though the contractor may be contractually bound to carry worker's comp, it won't hurt for you to insist on being shown the actual policy and checking the dates that it's in force.

Is there a termination clause?

☐ yes   ☐ no

We all start projects with high hopes and good humor. However, sometimes things don't work out. The contractor may simply not be doing things the way we want. Or he or she may be taking too long. Or the contractor may never even show up after the first day. If things go badly, how do you get out of the contract? There should be a termination clause explaining how either party can walk away. Sometimes these clauses are very specific. You don't pay on time, and the contractor's out of there (with a mechanic's lien on you for work already done). The contractor fails to show up as required on five consecutive days, and you have the right to bail out. Most contracts, however, simply leave it in the air and mention such things as attorney fees and arbitration. (See the following section.) It's usually to your advantage to have this spelled out as tightly as you can, and if possible, tied to an approval clause.

Is there an attorney's fees clause?   ☐ yes ☐ no

If things go really badly, attorneys will get involved. If that's the case, then there are going to be hefty fees to be paid. Who pays them? It's tempting to have a clause say that the losing party to a lawsuit is responsible for all the attorney's fees, including those of the other party. After all, you say to yourself, you'd only get involved if right was on your side, and in that case, you'd surely win. Maybe. Maybe not. Sometimes what seems perfectly obvious to you will not be so clear to a judge. You could lose . . . and then you'd be responsible for not only your fees, but the contractor's as well. (Think how much this would be if it's a treble attorney fee clause!) It's something to consider. Sometimes it's simply best to have each party pay his or her own lawyer.

Is there an arbitration clause?   ☐ yes ☐ no

Often, contracts will include a clause that says any dispute will automatically go to arbitration for settlement. The idea here is to avoid a lawsuit and high attorney fees. But what if the contractor rips apart your home and then walks away? You could be financially damaged for a lot of money. You may want to sue. Why give up your right to sue before you know the circumstances? After all, you and the contractor can always sign an arbitration agreement later on. And keep in mind that arbitration itself is not cheap. Arbitrators charge very high fees for their services. Check with your attorney.

Is the full price indicated?   ☐ yes ☐ no

As noted earlier, it's usually to your advantage to have a full-price contract. Somewhere there should be a bottom line on costs including materials and labor. It could be $1000 or $100,000, but that's what the job will cost, and barring any changes you make (see the prior question on changing plans), that's what it will cost you. Sometimes contractors underestimate the costs of doing the job. They may come to you and say they didn't know that it was going to cost so much to relocate plumbing, or to firm up flooring. They want more money. If there's a full price listed in the contract, it's now up to you. You can either pay them (and you probably should if the new expenses were unexpected and are real), or simply say, "No, I'll only pay what the contract specifies." Then it's up to the contractor to complete the job at a loss, do less expensive (and usually less satisfactory work), or simply walk away and dare you to come after him or her.

If it's a time and materials contract, is there a clause calling for renegotiation?

☐ yes ☐ no

With renovation, as noted earlier, because of the unknown nature of much of the work (tearing into existing walls and not knowing what you'll find), many contracts are for time and materials. However, that doesn't have to mean that you're on the hook for an unlimited amount of money. You may want to put in a maximum price. If that price is reached, then it's time to renegotiate. You may simply want to stop the work (usually a bad choice), or try something different. A renegotiation clause with a price trigger can give you this option.

Does the contract specify who will supply and pay for materials?

☐ yes ☐ no

In the previous chapter we discussed your options here: The contractor can do it all (usually the easiest method), you can do it all, or there can be a combination. To be sure that everyone is reading from the same page, the contract should clearly spell this out.

Is there a payment schedule?

☐ yes ☐ no

Are you planning on paying for the job in a lump sum? Or are you expected to pay in installments? The contract should specify exactly how payment is to be made. If it's an installment schedule, the contract should specify at what point a payment is to be made as well as how much. For example, if you're having kitchen work done, you may be expected to pay 30 percent upon installation of the cabinets, 30 percent upon installation of the counter-tops, and 30 percent when the remaining work is done, 10 percent being held over until the period for mechanic's liens runs out. (See the following section.)

Is there a holdback written into the contract? ☐ yes ☐ no

You may find that as soon as work is completed, the contractor will demand full satisfaction of payment. In other words, he or she wants all the rest of the money. But you may be concerned about mechanic's liens. You may want to hold back a percentage until the lien time has run out, or you're otherwise satisfied that there's no a problem. A holdback clause allows you to hang onto some of the money for a period of time. Without the clause, you probably owe it all upon job completion.

Will I be able to fulfill the payment schedule? ☐ yes ☐ no

If there's a payment schedule, it's important that you have the financial resources in hand when called upon to pay. It won't do to tell the contractor that you're still negotiating with the bank for a home equity loan, but that you expect the money in a week or so. You'll find that work on your job will come to a screeching halt. Be sure to arrange any needed financing well in advance so that you know you'll have the funds on hand when needed to make scheduled payments. It will make the contractor very happy, and you'll be much more at ease yourself.

Should I sign? ☐ yes ☐ no

I only sign a contract when I am fully convinced that it covers everything in the renovation, when I'm satisfied that my interests are fully covered, and when my financial advisor (usually an attorney) tells me it's okay to sign. I never sign if I don't understand a clause or some other portion of the contract, if I'm worried that the contract does not clearly express my wishes, or if I'm pressured to sign. Pressure can take the form of the contractor's offering to cut the price 20 percent, but only if I sign right now. If I wait until tomorrow, the price goes up. I'll never sign under that kind of pressure. Besides, almost always, the price tomorrow will still be the same as it was today.

Should I make payment when I sign? ☐ **yes** ☐ **no**

It depends on what your contract specifies. If you agree to pay a certain amount in advance of work being performed, then you will probably want to give that money to the contractor at the time of signing. If you don't, don't expect the contractor to begin work anytime soon. Keep in mind that for small jobs, contractors usually won't ask for any advance money. However, for larger jobs, the contractor may indeed want some up-front money, particularly if there are a lot of materials purchases involved.

Does the contract specify whether I'll be able to live in the home during renovation? ☐ **yes** ☐ **no**

You'll want the contract to spell out your living arrangements during the renovation period. For example, it might say that the contractor must keep your living quarters partitioned off from the work area. You may also specify that the contractor must make a reasonable effort to keep dust and dirt away from your living area and to control loud sounds. Keep in mind, however, that you're now involved in construction and noise; dust and dirt are simply part of the job. Even if the contract says these are to be kept down (no contractor worth his or her salt is dumb enough to say that all noise, dirt, and dust will be eliminated), it's going to be loud and dirty.

Questions to Ask Your Contractor

Will you agree to use my contract? ☐ **yes** ☐ **no**

Most contractors are very unwilling to use any contract but the one they come armed with. This is not because they mistrust you. It's because they don't trust themselves when it comes to reading the fine print and understanding what your contract will make them live up to. If it's a big job, the contractor will want to take it to someone to look over, presumably a lawyer or a trusted friend who understands legalese. This will take time and may cost him or her money, which will be reflected in a bigger bill to you. Sometimes the easiest way to handle this is to take the contractor's contract to your lawyer and have it modified as little as possible, then take it back to the contractor and explain clearly any changes you want and why. If what you want is reasonable and understandable, you probably can get agreement.

Is there any term in the contract you can't fulfill? ☐ **yes** ☐ **no**

A few contractors "play" their clients. They tell them what they want to hear. They sign whatever. Then, they go ahead and do exactly what they want. The contractor may full well know that there's no way to get the job done by Christmas, but will sign anyhow believing that as long as you see work progressing, you'll not hold to the date. Or there may be no way to get the particular tile or granite you want. But the contractor says that he or she will try. Don't let a contractor play this game with you. Ask up front if there are any terms that are unrealistic and simply can't be fulfilled. Better to get it out into the open now, before you sign and when you can modify things, than later on when you simply have to live with it.

Have you signed the contract? ☐ **yes** ☐ **no**

This may sound simpleminded, but a few contractors will take your signed version of the contract, tear out duplicates, and hand them to you without signing themselves. And some people either won't notice, won't care, or will go along with this. Be sure that the contractor has signed the final version of your contract. And if you've written in any changes, be sure that he or she has initialed them.

When do you want the first payment? ☐ **yes** ☐ **no**

The contractor may be expecting an initial payment upon signing, even if the contract does not call for one. Or he or she may be anticipating getting paid after the entire job is done, even though payment is specified in several disbursements. Just because it's written in the contract, don't think every contractor has read it carefully, or even has thought much about it. Most contractors these days are very busy, and a few may just zip through the contract as a formality. Be sure you've both agreed up front on when the first payment will be made (even if it's also the last payment).

When will you begin work?   ☐ yes   ☐ no

Your contract may have a start date. But that may have been set to give the contractor maximum leeway in getting to your job. Another job may fall through or be delayed, and the contractor may be able to start earlier than the start date. Of course, that may not be convenient with you if you're planning a house party two days after he or she plans to begin. Talk to the contractor about realistic times for beginning work. And keep in mind that if you can be flexible with time, often contractors can work you in early and get the job finished early.

What arrangements will you make for me to live in the home while work progresses?   ☐ yes   ☐ no

Regardless of how clear this is spelled out in the contract, it's also good to talk it through. What kind of temporary wall will the contractor build between the renovation work and the existing home where you'll be living? Will it be a sheet rock wall? Will it be insulated? Will it be a plastic drop curtain? Will the contractor have someone on the job to ensure that the dirt and dust getting into your area is minimal? Is the contractor planning on starting at a particular hour in the morning? Will you be up by then? What about toilet facilities—is the contractor planning on having the crew use your bathroom(s) or is a portable toilet being hauled in? A good conversation about these practical matters can avoid bruised feelings later on.

Will you begin work, then stop and start, or will you work continuously until finished?   ☐ yes   ☐ no

Some contractors work piecemeal. They may have three crews and 12 jobs. So they work for a time on one job, then switch to another. Too often they switch when some other owner complains. On the other hand, some contractors have one crew and handle one job at a time. They simply try to schedule their jobs end to end. The latter is the most satisfying contractor for most owners. It means that he or she will begin and then continue working right through to the end. However, this latter contractor may also be the most expensive.

Questions to Ask Your Attorney

Are there any additional clauses I should add to the contract?

☐ yes   ☐ no

Most attorneys won't want you to use the contractor's contract. Rather, they will prefer to draw their own. The problem, as we've seen, is that many contractors will be put off by this. The compromise is to have your attorney add clauses that are absolutely needed to the contractor's document. However, keep in mind that in their eagerness to protect you, many attorneys will go overboard and create such a one-sided contract that no renovator will be willing to sign it. Look over the clauses the attorney wants to add. Ask why they are necessary. See if some (or many) can be avoided.

What risks does the contract subject me to?

☐ yes   ☐ no

Just because an attorney looks it over and adds a few paragraphs doesn't mean the contract is risk free. There are always risks, particularly when you're dealing with unknown territory, as is the case with renovation. Ask your attorney to spell these out for you and what your recourses are. You may be surprised to learn how little your contract actually protects you and how much you're counting on the good will and good word of your contractor. It's something to think about.

What is a mechanic's lien?

☐ yes   ☐ no

Have your attorney explain the mechanic's lien laws in your state. All states have mechanic's lien laws, which allow suppliers of material and labor to place a lien (a money encumbrance, something that ties up your title) on your property if you don't pay. In some cases, liens can be very nasty, and the mechanic can force sale of your property in order to get his or her money! Be aware that mechanic's liens can have very strict deadlines and procedures that must be met both by the mechanic and by you. Miss a deadline and there might be no lien. Or you might lose your home! These are nothing to fool with—as I said, have your attorney give you a thorough explanation of those in your state.

Who can slap a mechanic's lien on me?

☐ yes ☐ no

Almost anyone at all who supplies labor or material can use a mechanic's lien. This can get very complicated. For example, your contractor may hire a subcontractor who may hire a plumber. You may pay your contractor, who in turn may pay the subcontractor, who for whatever reason may not pay the plumber. The plumber may then be able to slap a mechanic's lien on you. This, even though in good faith you paid your contractor and he or she in turn paid the sub! The tricky part about avoiding mechanic's liens is finding out who is supposed to pay whom, and who isn't getting paid. Ultimately, if it's your property, you're responsible for seeing that everyone gets paid. In some weird situations, that could mean paying for the same job twice!

What is the filing procedure for mechanic's liens?

☐ yes ☐ no

Every state is somewhat different. In California, whose rules some other states follow, it's a two-step procedure. A "prelim," or preliminary notice usually must be served to you before the lien can be filed a minimum of 20 days after you first receive materials or labor is performed. Thus, as soon as work starts you may suddenly get a handful of prelims from materials suppliers and subcontractors. They are simply notifying you that if you don't pay later on, they can slap you with a lien. In California, the subs and materials suppliers can file the lien up to 60 days after their work ends or 90 days after the whole project is completed. You can cut 30 days off both of these by filing a "notice of completion." Once the time limits are up, it's too late for the lien to be filed. The filing of a mechanic's lien theoretically needs an attorney; however, there are agencies available to help mechanics file liens on their own so the cost to them is limited . . . and it's easier for them to file!

Should I get releases to help avoid mechanic's liens? ☐ yes ☐ no

Mechanics can sign releases saying that they have been paid. Often, a general contractor will get lien releases from all the subs and hand them to you before asking for payment. However, these are almost always conditional releases. In other words, they release you provided that the mechanic actually does get paid. If the contractor you pay in turn doesn't pay the sub or supplier, you're still on the hook for a mechanic's lien. You can get an *unconditional* lien release. However, usually a mechanic will give it to you only after he or she has been paid and the check has cleared the bank.

Should I pay for labor and materials directly to avoid mechanic's liens? ☐ yes ☐ no

One method of trying to avoid mechanic's liens is to pay for all labor and materials directly yourself. You hand the check to the sub or the supplier, so you know that he or she got it. The trouble here is that this tends to undermine the authority of the general contractor and also sends the message that you don't entirely trust him or her. Many general contractors are insulted by this and won't work for you if they know that's what you intend to do. Besides, it's still often up to the general contractor to tell you exactly who has worked on the job and where materials were obtained.

Should I use two-party checks to avoid mechanic's liens? ☐ yes ☐ no

Yet another method of trying to avoid mechanic's liens that your attorney may suggest you do is to pay for everything using so-called voucher checks. Thus, the checks are made out to both the general contractor and the sub or supplier. Both must sign before the check can be cashed. Thus, the GC can't sign the check alone and run with the money. And once either the sub or supplier signs, you have your receipt that they've received the money. Of course, the sub or supplier can still say that the check didn't cover the full amount of the bill—only a portion, and more is yet due.

Is there anything else I should do to help avoid mechanic's liens?

☐ yes ☐ no

Your attorney may have some clever ideas that will work in your state. Keep in mind, however, that while mechanic's liens are a real threat, they happen fairly rarely in home renovation projects. Most often you're dealing directly with the person who's doing the work, and usually you have a personal relationship with him or her. Very often, the mechanic is counting on your references to get him or her future work. If you pay as agreed, chances are everything will go fine and you won't have anything to worry about. Nevertheless, still check it out with your attorney.

Should I sign the contract?

☐ yes ☐ no

This is what it all comes down to, what you're paying the attorney for. It's surprising that, when the question is put bluntly to them, some attorneys will hem and haw and add caveats such as if you understand the risks, and if you trust the contractor, and if we don't have sunspots, it's probably okay to sign. They don't want you coming back later if things go wrong and saying that it's their fault. Nevertheless, a good lawyer who has properly drawn up a renovation agreement for you should have no hesitation in telling you to sign it. If he or she hems and haws too much, or tells you not to sign, it could be time to look for another attorney.

3
Plans and Permissions

Questions to Ask Yourself

Have I checked out similar projects in magazines? ☐ yes ☐ no

It's important not to reinvent the wheel. No matter what your renovation project happens to be, chances are someone somewhere has done something similar. And chances are also good that it's been written up. Be sure to check all of the popular remodeling magazines (such as *Bedrooms and Baths, Home and Architectural Trends, Homestyle Home Plans, Interior Design, Taunton's Fine Home Building, This Old House,* and so on) that report, with pictures and sometimes plans, on clever and unique projects. You may find that someone already has handled a narrow kitchen such as yours in a way that you never anticipated. And you can incorporate those ideas in your own plans. Don't be shy about cutting interesting articles out of magazines and creating a folder for them that you can often refer to.

Have I checked out similar projects in showrooms? ☐ yes ☐ no

Many building supply stores, such as Home Depot, Lowes, and others, offer kitchen and bathroom setups. These demonstrate what can be done with various products. The advantage of visiting these places is that you can see first hand how something will look when finished. While a picture may be worth a thousand words, seeing it in person is worth a thousand pictures. Be sure not to overlook the many plumbing supply stores that will have displays of bathroom fixtures. And also check out stores that sell kitchen appliances–often they will show many models as set up in a typical kitchen, and you can quickly see how large (or small) they really are and the kind of looks they offer. Besides, for a small fee some of these stores will create three-dimensional renderings of what the products you choose will look like in your home for you.

Have I seen what's being done in model homes?   ☐ **yes**   ☐ **no**

Let the builders do your homework for you. Home-builders are constantly checking the latest innovations to see what's new. Many even conduct buyer surveys to find out what potential customers are thinking and what their preferences are. Whenever you get a chance, stop at the model homes for new construction. Take a few minutes to tour the site. Check out any areas that you may be thinking of renovating, and see how the new homes are handling it. You're sure to get loads of ideas. And in the process, you may even decide that it makes more sense to buy another home than it does to fix up the one you have!

Have I checked out manufacturer's sites online?   ☐ **yes**   ☐ **no**

Many manufacturers operate their own websites that include not only descriptions of their products (which in itself can be helpful) but also images of their products in homes. Some of the better sites include: *www.kohler.com* (kitchen and bath fixtures), *www.faucet.com* (faucets and other fixtures), *www.diamond2.com* (cabinets), *www.kraftmaid.com* (cabinets), *www.merilat.com* (cabinets), *www.daltile.com* (tile). In addition, *www.buildingonline.com* and *www.build.com* are search engines that can link you to other home renovation sites. Also, don't forget to check out *www.nari.org,* the site for the National Association of the Remodeling Industry.

Have I checked out builders' sites on the Internet?   ☐ **yes**   ☐ **no**

Many builders who specialize in renovation now have Internet sites. If you check out their web pages, you can not only learn about what they specialize in, but also often get images of their latest efforts. It's only as far away as your computer and browser. Use a good search engine (such as *Google.com*) and try keywords such as "renovator," "home renovation," and "remodeling." Be sure to also key in your area or city, or else you'll get sites from London, England to Seoul, Korea!

Have I started watching building shows on TV?   ☐ **yes**   ☐ **no**

Home renovation has become big business since the turn of the century and the boom in residential housing. Televisions shows, from the classic *This Old House* to *Home-Time*, detail not only want you can do to your house, but how to do it. Most of the shows have websites, and you can check these out for old shows on a subject that you're interested in, such as bathrooms. Then you can send in for a tape of the show.

Have I called in several contractors for ideas?   ☐ **yes**   ☐ **no**

If you're not sure exactly how to begin, why not call a professional? Most renovation contractors are happy to come out, evaluate your home, and give you their ideas on what will work best. Remember, these are the people who do it day in and day out, so their advice is based in practical experience. You may have elaborate ideas of taking out a wall and converting an unneeded bedroom into extra living space. However, the contractor can take a look and quickly determine that the wall between is load-bearing and that it would be impractical, not to mention cost a fortune, to do the work you anticipate. He or she usually can also give you alternative ideas.

Have I asked for advice from an interior decorator?   ☐ **yes**   ☐ **no**

Interior decorators help you buy appropriate furniture, right? What could they possibly know about renovations? The answer is that they see homes all the time, probably many like yours, in before and after states. Not only can they tell you what furniture will fit, but sometimes they can tell you which renovation ideas will work, and which will produce ghastly results. And they may even be able to direct you to homes where the owners have done the work, so you can see for yourself. You may have to pay here, although some department stores run a complimentary service.

Have I consulted with an architect?

☐ yes   ☐ no

Most of us think of architects as people who design build-ings from the ground up. Of course, they do that too, but many architects are more than willing to consult with you on a renovation project. They usually have good ideas for what the final results should look like. And they may come up with some highly creative ideas you'd never think of yourself. Finally, if you like their ideas, they can not only draw sketches, but can come up with a set of working plans that any good contractor can follow. How-ever, architects generally do not work cheaply. It might easily cost you a grand or more to get one out to your home to write up some ideas. (And that's before the plans!) However, it could be money very well spent.

Have I drawn a sketch?

☐ yes   ☐ no

You undoubtedly have your own ideas of what you'd like done. If it's just replacing old cabinets with new in the same arrangement, then you probably don't need a plan. But if you want to take advantage of the many new types of cabinetry that are available, or you have some other redesign work in mind, then you should put together your own sketch—draw it out. No, you don't need to be an artist; you just need to be able to get it close enough so that someone else can see what you have in mind. No matter how simple the concept may be, you'll find it far easier to get the idea across to someone else when it's down on paper.

Can I save money drawing my own working plans?

☐ yes   ☐ no

Of course, after you've finalized what your plans are, you may need a set of working drawings that the contractor can follow. An architect can draw these up for you, but expect to pay thousands more. On the other hand, some owners draw them up themselves. The problem here is that these plans need to include the details about what you want done as well as follow certain conventions used in the building trades. If you've worked with contractors before, know what blueprints look like, and have a good working knowledge of drafting, there's no reason why you can't come up with your own plans that will be acceptable both to a building department and to a contractor. If you're new to this, on the other hand, let a pro draw up the plans for you. It will cost a bit more, but you'll save a lot of headaches.

Have I considered using a draftsman?   ☐ yes   ☐ no

On the other hand, you may only need a set of working plans or a more detailed drawing based on your own crude renderings. Why hire a luxury limousine when a taxicab will do? There are many draftsmen out there who do nothing other than come up with renderings and working plans. They can be found in the phone book, and for a few hundred dollars, they may be able to turn out just what you need.

Have I consulted with an engineer?   ☐ yes   ☐ no

If you're going to do any sort of room rearrangement or addition, you may need to check with an engineer. Anytime you change the roofline, the foundation, or the support walls, you should have the plans engineered. Here the engineer takes a look at the snow load (very important in northern states), the wind (important in southern states), and other factors in order to determine the size and strength of building materials to be used. For example, should that beam be a two-by-eight or a four-by-eight? Should the studs be two-by-four or two-by-six? And so on. A structural engineer will tell you. Some building departments require an engineering stamp before approving any new work.

Have I checked out materials costs at building stores?   ☐ yes   ☐ no

Once you get a list of the materials you'll need, it's wise to check out just how much they'll cost. Be sure your list is thorough, from the kitchen sink down to the boards and nails you need. Also keep in mind that if you use a contractor, he or she may be able to get the same materials (or at least most of them) at a substantial discount. Be sure to ask the contractor to pass those savings on to you.

Do I need a land survey?

☐ yes   ☐ no

Probably not, if you're not going to change the outside periphery of your home. On the other hand, if you're doing an addition that involves breaking new ground, then you should get a survey. This will give you the exact boundaries of your property. Keep in mind that most communities require that you maintain specific setbacks from your neighbors. Typically, this is 5 to 15 feet on the sides, and 20 or more feet in the back. You will not be able to put up an addition into these areas. Of course, you need to know where the boundaries are in order to maintain the setbacks. (Don't simply rely on a fence between two properties. These are notoriously wrong, often placed by eye, and may be a few feet one way or the other on yours or your neighbor's yard!)

Have I shown my plans to real estate agents?

☐ yes   ☐ no

Once you have a set of plans that someone else can read, show them around. If you have a friend who is an agent, show him or her the plans. Ask them what they think. I was once considering taking out the fourth bedroom of a home in order to increase the living area. The agent was aghast telling me that four bedroom homes were in great demand in the area. I'd actually be cutting the value of my home by doing the renovation work! An agent will give you practical marketing advice. If you don't know an agent, simply call one. Most are very happy to come out and give you any advice they can on the hope that when you sell, you'll list with them.

Have I shown my plans to friends, relatives and associates?

☐ yes   ☐ no

People who know you can often give you very useful, personal advice. They may be able to take one look and say, "You're not going to be happy with the changes." They may point to a long, dark hallway you're creating and note that you've never liked hallways. However, in your eagerness to come up with a set of plans that work in the existing house, you may have compromised yourself in a long hallway. Seeing it through their eyes can help you determine if the changes are what you truly want.

Do I need approval from my homeowner's association?   ☐ yes   ☐ no

While all condos belong to a homeowner's association (HOA), many single-family homes do also. If your home is part of an HOA, you should assume that you need their approval to make any external changes to your property. (You probably don't need their approval for any changes that don't show from the street or from neighbors' homes.) Such changes can run the gamut from landscaping the front to making structural changes to the your home. (In a condo, you should assume that you cannot make any external changes; it's a rare HOA that would allow you to do so.) Usually there is a simple procedure to be followed—a form to fill out and submit along with sketches and drawings. Don't expect automatic approval. Many HOAs are loath to allow changes to the neighborhood and are prepared to fight tooth and nail to maintain the status quo.

Will the HOA require me to do the job within a certain time frame?   ☐ yes   ☐ no

Usually they will. Typically, the HOA will insist that all the work be done within six months to a year. If you do not start the work by that time, your permission will expire, and you will probably need to reapply. Be sure to pay attention to HOA deadlines. Just because you applied once and got permission, doesn't mean you'll get it again. There may be a new architectural committee (that passes on such things) or the existing one may have new ideas. Once you get permission, go with it. And if you can't complete in time, ask for extensions.

Does the HOA impose any working conditions limitations?   ☐ yes   ☐ no

Typically they do. They may insist on your keeping the site clean at all times. They may require that you not put building materials or dumpsters in the street in front of your home for more than, for example, 72 hours. They may require that your workpeople keep the noise down—no loud radios, which is often a frequent complaint. They may require that you notify neighbors well in advance if you're going to do any heavy duty work such as blasting, structural tear down, and the like, or if you're bringing in any heavy machinery such as a crane to lift a roof joist into place.

Do I need a building permit?   ☐ yes   ☐ no

You usually do. If the work you're doing is strictly painting or minor changing of fixtures or appliances, you may not need a permit. But the minute you get into anything structural, electrical, plumbing, or the like, a permit is mandatory. Don't make the mistake of thinking that you can skip the permitting process because no one will know. When you sell, you'll need to disclose to the buyer whether or not the work was done with a permit. If it wasn't, it could adversely affect your sale. Also, should there be a fire or other problem, your homeowner's insurance may not want to pay off if you did work without the benefit of a permit.

Will I pull the permit?   ☐ yes   ☐ no

Either you or your contractor can pull the permits. Since this often involves waiting an hour or more down at city hall, you can save yourself some costs by doing it yourself. If your contractor does it, he or she will simply bill you for the time. Keep in mind that in some communities, you will *not* be allowed to do certain work yourself. For example, the permit may specify that all work involving electricity or gas *must* be done by a professional. Other communities are more liberal and may allow you to do any work you choose on your own home, provided that you agree to live in the property afterward for a period of time, typically a year. Very few building departments will let you do your own permitted work and then turn around and immediately sell the home. To protect the next buyer, they want the work done by professionals.

How many permits will I need?   ☐ yes   ☐ no

If you've never pulled permits before, you'll be surprised to learn how many there are. In addition to a general permit for overall construction, you may also be required to get electrical, mechanical (duct work), plumbing, or other specialty permits. (Actually there can be dozens of different permits required!) In order to get a permit, you will almost always be required to present a set of plans or at the least a sketch of what you intend to do. (You do not normally need formal plans—as long as the department can visualize what you have in mind, they can determine if you'll get a permit and what kind.) Based on your sketch or plans, the building department will tell you which permits you need.

How much will the permits cost?   ☐ **yes**   ☐ **no**

If this is your first time, you may be surprised at how costly permits can be. A permit to put in a new 220-volt line for a spa you want to add to your back yard could cost you a hundred dollars or more. Permits for a major addition to your house could cost hundreds if not thousands of dollars. There are several reasons for the expense. The permits may include plan checks by building department engineers. They typically include as many physical inspections as are necessary to approve the work. They may also include taxes (in the case of major renovation) to support other entities, such as fire departments or schools. And finally, the city may get some of its operating revenues from the permits. There's usually nothing you can do about the amount. You'll just have to build it into your renovation costs.

What should I do if my plan is turned down?   ☐ **yes**   ☐ **no**

Don't panic. It's a rare set of plans that isn't turned down, at least the first time. Building departments mainly adhere to the UBC (Uniform Building Code), but may also have their own specific requirements. If you're new to this, it's very unlikely you'll meet all their technical requirements the first time out. At the plan check, the building department engineer will usually highlight in red all areas of your plans that need correction, and may suggest what those corrections should be. If you're uncertain about what is wanted, you should ask a staff member, who will typically take the time to explain how the building department wants the work done. If you then simply comply with their wishes, you'll get your plan approved. Problems occur when what you want and what the building department wants are two different things.

Do I need planning department approval?

☐ **yes** ☐ **no**

Maybe. The planning department looks at the use of the property. For example, they are concerned that a gas station isn't built in the middle of a residential tract. They are also concerned about the size and use of your home. For example, zoning laws may demand single-family use in your area, and you want to convert your home to a duplex or for double-family use. You would need to get a variance from the planning commission. In the absence of a home owner's association, the planning commission may also enforce the CC&Rs (Covenants, Conditions, and Restrictions) that run with your property, which may determine the appearance of your home, even the color you can paint it. Usually, the building department will tell you if you need planning department approval, but sometimes you'll just need to check it out yourself.

What do I do if the planning department or commission turns me down?

☐ **yes** ☐ **no**

After the first turndown (yes, this could be a drawn out process!), you may need to come back requesting a variance. This means that your plans don't meet the requirements of the city's master plan or zoning laws, and you'd like a one-time, one-location exception made. Typically, your request will have to go before the entire planning commission. Their purpose is to maintain zoning laws and the master plan, so you will need to show why your variance will not adversely affect either. If you can bring neighbors (or a petition signed by them) showing that they're in favor (or at least not against) your proposal, it will usually help. Your chance of success depends on how radical the changes are that you want to make and how liberal the commission is. Unfortunately, most people do not succeed, at least the first time. The commission may make suggestions for changes to your plans that will bring it more in line with what the city wants, and after going back and forth several times, you may actually get your variance.

Have I checked with the front desk at the planning department?   ☐ yes   ☐ no

While the previous questions address the formal procedure for getting a variance, there is an informal procedure that could work as well, if not better. Typically, there is a front desk for the planning commission, and you can bring your plans there for approval. However, instead of simply dropping them off, ask to show them to a staff member. See what the reaction is. Often the staff will explain problems with your plans, and you can negotiate back and forth until you get a more acceptable plan. Then ask if the staff will recommend it to the planning commission. More often than not, staff-recommended plans get approval.

How long am I willing to wait for approval?   ☐ yes   ☐ no

If your plans require a variance, or if the building department doesn't approve them and requires significant changes, you could be set back to ground zero. You might have to start over. Since the building department may take several weeks initially to give you a response (depending on the complexity of what you want to do and their back-load), and the planning commission, which typically meets monthly, make take longer, it could be quite a while before you get necessary approvals, even if there are no problems. If there are problems, it can drag out interminably. I have seen the approval process last over a year, until ultimately, either the owner was successful, or simply gave up.

How many resources am I willing to commit to getting approval?   ☐ yes   ☐ no

While there is usually no or only a nominal charge for a planning commission approval, and we've already discussed building plan fees, there could be other expenses. Each time you are knocked down and have to come back, it could require a new set of plans, and the cost for these will not be cheap. Additionally, you may need to spend your time (which is money) in getting neighbors to come out in your support (or at least to sign a petition). And if it turns into a real slugfest, there are always the attorney fees. It's a good idea at the beginning to determine just how much time, energy, and money you're willing to devote to getting your dream renovation approved. As some point, you may determine that it's either better just to fold your tent and steal away into the night, or scale down what you hoped to do.

Questions to Ask Your Architect

How quickly can you complete the plans?   ☐ **yes**   ☐ **no**

While the actual work may only take a few days or less, it might be far longer before the architect can get to it. Just a few years ago, when renovations were done infrequently, you could expect to get your plans back within a few weeks. However, as of this writing with millions of renovations being done each year, the available architects (and draftsmen) are hard pressed to keep up with the load. I recently wanted to get a set of plans, and was told the waiting time was 16 months! Hopefully, your architect can get to your plans sooner.

Can you incorporate cost-saving changes?   ☐ **yes**   ☐ **no**

Part of what you pay an architect for is to cost-design your renovation. Because he or she presumably has done this many times before and has a good knowledge of the renovation process as well as materials, the architect should be able to make suggestions that will cut your costs. Sometimes these savings can be high enough to cover the entire fees of the architect. (That's something to consider when you're trying to decide whether or not to call one in.)

How much will it cost for me to change your plans?   ☐ **yes**   ☐ **no**

The old joke about renovation is that plans are never final; they are always being redrawn. The reason, of course, is that as the existing structure is demolished, new problems occur requiring new solutions . . . and, you've got it, new plans. So this is an important question to ask your architect or draftsperson. Sometimes it's better to pay more initially with the right to have the plans redrawn several times without (or at minimal) cost, than to pay separately for each occurrence. The question usually is not whether you'll need to have your plans redrawn, but how many times.

Will you handle any engineering required?   ☐ yes   ☐ no

If you're doing structural changes, particularly those involving roofs, ceilings, foundations, or support walls, you'll need to have your plans engineered (as noted in earlier sections). Many architects are capable of handling this themselves, and will do so. Some draftsmen are not. Be sure you ask. If you need to have your plans taken to an outside civil engineering firm, you'll have to pay hundreds of dollars extra.

Will you provide me with a full set of renderings and working plans?   ☐ yes   ☐ no

This may seem obvious, but it's not. Your ultimate goal is to have accurate sketches and plans of your renovation project that you can submit to your contractor for bid and to your building department for permits. On the other hand, architects have different fee structures. Renderings may be so much per picture, plans may be another cost, and working plans (which include separate segments for plumbing, electrical, structural, and so on) another. Be sure you're getting what you want and that you know how much it will cost.

Questions to Ask Your Builder

Can you suggest any changes to the plans that will save me money or make construction more efficient?   ☐ yes   ☐ no

Contractors who do renovation work for a living have learned a host of shortcuts. Some of these can save you a lot of money. Others you may want to skip because of the compromises to your plan that they require. In any event, you should show your contractor your sketch or plans and ask if there are changes he or she can suggest that will save you money. Almost always the contractor will suggest several things. Some of these may simply be to make his or her job easier, which can translate to cost savings. Others may be design changes, which can save in materials costs. And yet others may involve rethinking the whole concept of what you want to do. However, unless you ask, you won't get the benefit of the contractor's experience.

Do you already have a set of plans I can use?

☐ yes ☐ no

If you live in a tract home that is one of many similar models, sometimes the contractor will have worked on your neighbor's home. And because the homes are similar, you may want to renovate something the same way your neighbor did. The contractor may already have a set of working plans. If you use these, you can save oodles of money. You'll save not only because you won't need to get plans from scratch, but because the contractor has already done similar work in a similar house and knows what he or she is likely to run into. This can translate into a much leaner bid.

Will you pull the permits for me?

☐ yes ☐ no

Trust me, if you're new to this, it's so much easier to have the contractor pull the permits. He or she, presumably, has done it a hundred times before, knows the people down at the building department, knows which permits to get, and knows how to fill out the forms. Further, if there's a problem with the plans or sketches, often the contractor can fix it right on the spot with the cooperation of the staff at the building department. If you're pulling the plans, you'll probably need to take them back to the contractor for consultations. Having the builder do it is the easy way to go. However, it's also more costly as the contractor will bill you for time spent.

How much extra will you charge to handle permits? When will you take care of it?

☐ yes ☐ no

As noted, it's also the expensive way. It's going to take the contractor away from his or her other work to get the permits. And he or she isn't going to like that. So contractors will often wait until they have several reasons to go down to the building department–your job, questions on another job, another set of plans, and so on. Thus, asking the contractor to do it could take extra time, sometimes weeks. Also, the contractor isn't going to do it for free. Ask him or her how much extra this is going to cost. If the contractor puts a figure on it, you may want to ask him or her to subtract that much from the bid if you do it yourself.

Questions to Ask Your Home Owner's Association

Do you require approval for the work I want to do? ☐ yes ☐ no

Don't assume that they do or that they don't. The general rule is that any changes to the outside of a building require HOA approval. Any changes to the inside do not. However, if you have a townhouse or condo in a multihome building, even changes inside, especially to electrical, plumbing, or other home systems, may require HOA approval. The best way to find out is to ask. In some HOAs, you can simply call the general manager. In others, all requests must be submitted formally in writing. Find out how it's done, and do it. It could save you a grievance later on.

How long do you take to give approval? ☐ yes ☐ no

Some HOAs are quite active and on the ball. They'll get your approval back to you within a week. Others are poorly managed and may rely all or partly on volunteers. It might take them a month or longer to give your approval. You may find, in fact, that you need to camp outside one of the architectural committee's member's homes in order to get anything done. On the other hand, the less organized the HOA, the less likely it is to get on your case if you don't follow your plans exactly as you proposed.

Do I need to go before the board or the architectural committee?   ☐ yes   ☐ no

In some organizations, everything is handled by the board of directors. This is sometimes also the case with co-ops. In other cases, the architectural committee wants all proposals to be presented to them in person by the owner. That means that if you want to make renovation changes, you may have to go before a board.

What is the best way to present my proposal?   ☐ yes   ☐ no

Ask the general manager what the procedure is. My own suggestion is that, at least for the initial meeting, you go by yourself (or with supporting neighbors), and if possible, with your architect and contractor. The board will ask you questions. You answer truthfully and use the architect and/or contractor to handle technical issues. It is a session where mutual respect should reign, and with any luck you'll get your way. On the other hand, too many times I've seen owners come down with their lawyers who try to lay the law down to the board. This usually results in board members' getting their backs up and refusing to pass anything. Try the carrot before you resort to the stick.

What conditions, if any, will you apply?   ☐ yes   ☐ no

Boards may pass your proposal as is, or with conditions. Be sure that you get the conditions from them in writing. Have the board president or the general manager sign the list of the conditions. That way they can't add to it as your work progresses. Also, as you fulfill the conditions, you can have a board member or the general manager check them off. Be sure you get a signature or initials each time.

How long do I have to complete the work?   ☐ yes   ☐ no

HOAs will typically give you a time limit, often six months to a year. Be sure to ask, and get in writing, exactly how long you have. Also ask if you can get extensions if the work isn't quite finished in time. Usually the board is quite willing to go along any way it can, as long as it feels you're being cooperative and not trying to do something without permission.

Questions to Ask the Building Department

What is your procedure for submitting plans for approval?

☐ yes ☐ no

If you're going to pull your own permits, go right up to the front desk and ask how it's done. Private citizens come up every day and pull their own permits. Almost always there are staff members who will take the time to explain the procedures. Usually, they'll show you a stack of permit applications, and after you explain what you want to do, indicate which you need to fill out. They'll also tell you what other supporting materials you may need to get the permit.

Can I use my own sketches? Can I do the work myself?

☐ yes ☐ no

The general rule is that you can use any kind of sketch or plan as long as it clearly shows both the existing structure and any changes you want to make. Thus, your own drawing, in theory, should work fine. But you should ask, just to be sure that your building department doesn't have some more stringent requirement. Similarly, with the exception of working with gas and electricity, most building departments will let you do your own work. But you should ask just to be sure. If they require professionals to do part or all of the work, it will significantly impact your plans.

What is the inspection schedule, and how to I request inspections?

☐ yes ☐ no

In order to get your work passed, it must be inspected. The building department will send out an inspector on at least two occasions. The first will be when the rough work is done (framing, rough plumbing, electrical, mechanical, and so on). The second inspection is when the work is completed and you're given a "final." Of course, depending on the complexity of the job, many other inspections in between may be required. Be sure that you know the procedure for getting an inspection. Typically, you need to call a special number by a certain time the day before you want an inspection in order to get it scheduled. This is the kind of detailed information you need.

What is the cost?   ☐ yes   ☐ no

Usually the fees for permit, plan-check, and inspections are not broken down separately. Rather, you pay a single fee. There may be an additional fee for a school, fire service, or other tax. Be sure you ask what the fees are, and also be sure you're willing and able to pay for them. Otherwise, the first time you'll hear about the fees is when you're presented with a bill and told to pay it at the cashier.

Is there some way to modify my plans to reduce the fees?   ☐ yes   ☐ no

Work with the staff at the building department on this. It may be that with a few simple changes, you can modify your plans so that you don't need so many permits. Or you may not need to pay taxes or other fees *if* you make certain critical changes. Yes, the staff is busy. But they're usually not too busy to help you if you are courteous, determined, and know exactly what questions to ask.

How long do I have to complete the work?   ☐ yes   ☐ no

Be sure you find out. Some building departments give you 90 days. For others, it's six months or more. Be sure you know how long you've got. And either meet the deadline, or apply for an extension. If you let the deadline lapse and go in late, you could be required to go back to *start*, apply for the permits all over again, and worst of all, pay the fees a second time. Deadlines are important in home renovation. Find out what they are . . . and observe them.

4
Financing the Work

Questions to Ask Yourself

Should I pay cash for the work?

☐ yes ☐ no

While accurate statistics are hard to come by, the consensus in the industry is that nearly half of all renovation work done by homeowners is paid for in cash. The owner takes the money out of savings or from other sources. If you are in the enviable position of being able to pay cash for your work, you might want to consider the advantages: no payments, no hassling with a lender, an easier time with a contractor (and sometimes, a lower bid!). Of course, once you spend the money on the renovation work, you won't have it to spend elsewhere.

Do I need the cash for other things?

☐ yes ☐ no

While you may have a fat savings account in the bank that keeps tempting you, you should first ask yourself if that money is committed elsewhere. Do you need it for your children's education? For your retirement? For health needs? For some other important purpose? Just because you have the money in an account, that doesn't mean it's disposable. You might have set it aside years ago, and now you don't really think much about the reason. But that reason may still be there. The rule to follow is don't spend money you've committed elsewhere. As soon as you do, chances are your original need will pop up. And you'll feel very foolish . . . and needy.

52

Will I be drawing down on a retirement or insurance account?

☐ yes   ☐ no

Many people look at that fat IRA or 401K or whole life insurance policy or other retirement or insurance account and dream about using the money for a renovation. You probably can borrow most of it out at next to no interest, and voila, you've got the funds for your renovation. Check with your financial advisor before you use that money. He or she may tell you that it's a good use of a low-interest-rate loan. On the other hand, your advisor may point out that if interest rates are low when you read this, you may be better off financing the renovation work using your house as collateral and paying it back monthly. One of the dangers with taking money out of retirement or insurance accounts is that you could be tempted not to pay it back in a timely fashion. And that could cause you to lose the insurance or to pay hefty penalties.

Have I decided to borrow the money?

☐ yes   ☐ no

The first step is making the commitment to yourself. With the way prices of homes have shot up in recent years, the chances are excellent that you'll be able to get some sort of financing for your renovation project. Thus, the big decision now is whether you actually want to do it. To help make this decision, you should find out what current interest rates on a variety of loan types are and how big your monthly payment will be. Keep in mind that in most cases the interest on the money you borrow can be tax deductible. (Check with your accountant on this.)

Have I checked with a mortgage broker?

☐ yes   ☐ no

In the old days when you wanted a mortgage you first went to a savings and loan institution. Today your first choice should be a mortgage broker. When it's a first mortgage, a good mortgage broker can give you a variety of options usually featuring the lowest interest rates and payments. A mortgage broker is particularly useful when you want to refinance your entire mortgage. Many can also handle smaller secondary financing such as "home equity loans." If you don't have a mortgage broker, check with a real estate agent you rely upon or with friends who have had good experiences. You can also look under "mortgage broker" (not mortgage banker, which is different) in the yellow pages.

Have I checked with a bank? ☐ yes ☐ no

As local banks have ceded much of the first-mortgage refinance business to mortgage brokers, many have expanded into making home equity and home renovation loans. Today, these typically second (or sometimes third) mortgages are readily available from banks. Your own bank is a good starting place, but with the market so competitive, you should also comparison shop at other banks as well. Remember, money is money and the lender who charges the least, all else being equal, is the one to use.

Have I checked with my credit union? ☐ yes ☐ no

If you belong to a credit union, be sure to shop for financing there. Credit unions will sometimes offer rates that are slightly lower to their members. They may also offer expedited applications and funding. If you are not currently a member of a credit union, but you have access to joining one through your work or some other organization, you may want to do so. The relatively minor fees that they may charge to join may be more than offset by the savings on financing that they offer.

Have I checked the Internet? ☐ yes ☐ no

These days, you can get a loan just as fast (sometimes much faster) over the Internet. Although much of the applying can be done online, federal guidelines normally require that you actually talk to a representative and physically sign the documents in the presence of a notary. There may also be additional requirements for dealing with financing online. Some online services include: *eloan.com*, *mortgage.com*, and *lendingtree.com*. When applying online, be very sure that you are clear about what you want *before* you get started.

Do I have some other source of borrowed funds?

☐ yes   ☐ no

If you have other assets, it may be cheaper and easier to borrow against them. For example, you can often get a very low-interest-rate loan against money in a bank account, stocks, insurance policies (noted previously), and so on. If you are renovating with the intention of selling afterward, you will probably only need the money for a short time. If it's for a very short time, one method (though not necessarily the cheapest way) to get the money may be to use your credit cards. Keep in mind that with most credit cards, the best thing to do is to buy materials with the card. Whenever you get cash advances, the interest typically begins immediately. Also, the cash-advance portion of the card usually has much tighter limits.

Have I considered discounts and rebates from utility companies?

☐ yes   ☐ no

Depending on what your project involves, you may be able to get discounts and/or rebates from your utility companies. These are typically available when you install additional insulation, buy energy-saving appliances; replace old air conditioners, space heaters, or water heaters; replace old single-pane with double-pane windows; install weather-stripping; and so forth. The good part is that this is not a loan–it's a direct payment to you. The bad part is that you usually have to jump through a lot of hoops to get it, sometimes including applying before you actually do the work. But the payoffs can be huge, as high as 50 percent or more of the total cost of the qualifying renovation.

Have I considered a home equity loan?

☐ yes   ☐ no

A home equity loan is often a good choice for renovation because it typically does not charge interest on the money until you actually use it. And because most are set up as second mortgages in the form of revolving accounts, you can pay back the money at any time without any penalty. Further, you are usually not restricted as to how you want to use the money. You can use it for renovation or to take a cruise. Just be sure that when you set up your home equity account, it's for enough money to complete the job. Most lenders won't grant these loans for more than 80 percent LTV (loan to value), meaning that your combined regular mortgage plus the home equity loan cannot be more than 80 percent of the value of your property.

Have I considered a home renovation loan?   ☐ yes   ☐ no

A home renovation loan is like a home equity loan except that you must use the money for a specific purpose, a home renovation project. The choice of projects is usually very liberal. And the interest cost of the financing may be slightly less than for a home equity loan. Also, in some cases, you can finance up to 100 percent of your LTV (loan to value). The downside is that in many cases the money is released only as you complete the work. This makes it a bit more difficult to work with a contractor.

Have I considered a government-insured loan?   ☐ yes   ☐ no

These are offered through banks, credit unions, and mortgage bankers. Using FHA Title I, you can get financing for 100 percent of LTV; the interest rates are competitive, and funding is similar to a home renovation loan. The maximum amount, however, is only $25,000. HUD's (Housing and Urban Development) 203(K) provides for money both to purchase and rehabilitate a home. Of course, there are strict requirements and limitations. For more information, check into *www.hud.gov* (home renovations).

Have I considered a whole-house refinance?   ☐ yes   ☐ no

Sometimes the quickest way to get good financing is simply to get an entire new first mortgage. The reason is that second mortgages (whether they be home renovation, home equity, or whatever) typically charge higher than market rates for first mortgagees. If you already have a first mortgage that's at or above the current market interest rate, why not refinance the entire mortgage for enough to pay off your existing loan and take out money to cover your refinance? You can readily find these loans for up to 80 percent LTV. Even higher percentages are available, but it then becomes more difficult to take money out. Nevertheless, a good mortgage broker can often combine a new first mortgage with a construction loan to get you the money you need. Remember, after your renovation work, your house will presumably be worth more than before. And this can be calculated into the amount of the financing.

Do I want long-term or short-term financing? ☐ yes ☐ no

It's important to understand your goals. Are you planning to live in the property for the rest of your life? Or are you renovating now in order to sell soon for a better price? The answer you give will help determine the type of financing you go for. (Keep in mind that nationally, most people sell their homes and move every seven to nine years.) If you are planning on staying for the long run, it makes more sense to get long-term financing, such as getting a new first mortgage to pay off your existing mortgage and cover the remodeling costs (see previous section). On the other hand, if you're planning to fix up and quickly resell, then getting short-term financing, even using credits cards, may be workable.

Do I have a maximum payment I can be comfortable with? ☐ yes ☐ no

When you apply for financing, whether it be a 30-year mortgage or a short-term home renovation loan, the lender will tell you how big a payment you can afford. This is based on formulas derived from looking at the histories of borrowers over the past 50 years. Most people are surprised at how big a payment the lender says they can make. It's often far more than you will feel comfortable with. If that's the case, my suggestion is that you throw the lender's calculations out the window and go with your instincts. Go with the highest payment that makes you feel comfortable, even if it means scaling back your renovation project a bit. It's better to sleep well at night in a slightly smaller, less fancy home, than to be up pacing the mansion floors worried about money.

Have I compared interest rates and payments? ☐ yes ☐ no

While we are all mainly concerned about the monthly payment and how big (or small) it's going to be, it's important to understand that this is largely a function of the interest rate. And that depends on financial market conditions. As this book is being written, interest rates are at historic lows. However, that won't last. They will go up and when they do, the monthly payment will go up as well. One way to reduce the monthly payment is to vary the length of the loan. Traditionally, the longer the term (the more payments you spread the loan over), the lower the payment. However, recently lenders have been offering to reduce the interest rate if you take a shorter-term mortgage, 7, 5, or 3 years, with payments calculated as if it were for 30 years. The lower interest rate lowers the payment. At the end of that short term, however, you have a "balloon payment" meaning you either have to refinance, or sell the house to pay off the mortgage. Other lenders offer adjustable rate mortgages, where the interest rate will fluctuate with market conditions. It could be low today and high tomorrow. The rule I follow is to get a fixed rate loan for the longest term when interest rates are low, to lock them in. Get a short term or adjustable rate mortgage when rates are high, and then refinance when they fall.

Have I compared other mortgage costs?   ☐ yes   ☐ no

Be well aware that there will be costs in applying for financing. These include the credit check, appraisal for the house, title insurance, and escrow fees, to name only a few. However, today many lenders build these costs into the interest rate. In other words, they increase the interest rate and then tell you there are no additional charges. This is often the case with many first mortgages and with home renovation and home equity loans issued by banks. Don't be fooled, however. The costs are there. The lenders can get them reduced because they do such a large volume of business, but they are never truly zero. You either pay them up front in fees, have them built into the interest rate, or have them included in the mortgage (by borrowing an additional amount to cover the costs). Be sure you take this into account when you compare different mortgages.

What will closing costs come to?   ☐ yes   ☐ no

Lenders are supposed to give you a fairly accurate estimate when you apply. Sometimes it's right on the money.

Sometimes it's miles off. Be sure that you know what these closing costs are and that you are prepared to pay them. Your best bet to ensure that the costs at closing are the same as those when you applied for the mortgage is to keep your options open—be prepared to delay your renovation project and to apply to a different lender if things don't go exactly as they were supposed to. To be able to do that means not giving the lender any money up front. My suggestion is that you never pay points or other fees (with the exception of the costs for appraisal and credit report) to the lender until you're ready to close the financing. That way, in case things turn out different than promised, you can walk away and look elsewhere with minimal financial damage to yourself.

Who will the lender write the check to? ☐ yes ☐ no

Ideally, you want the funds from the loan to go directly to you. Then, at your discretion, you can pay the contractor, the subs, the materials suppliers, and so on. This gives you maximum control. However, some lenders, particularly if you have a home renovation loan or a construction loan, will not want the check written to you. They will want to write the check directly to the contractor(s) and the materials suppliers. In this way, they will know that the appropriate people have been paid. If that's the case, insist that the lender write a two-party check–to both you and the other person—written in such a way that it takes two signatures to cash. In this fashion, you can still retain some control over the project. Note: Some states will not allow the check to be directly written to the contractor alone.

Can the borrowing be handled as a construction loan? ☐ yes ☐ no

A construction loan is intended primarily for new buildings. It's arranged primarily through banks. To get it, you submit the working plans, the qualifications of the contractor, as well as the usual information about yourself for loan qualifying. When granted, the bank gives you a certain amount of time, typically a year or less, to finish construction. Funds are released in installments as work is completed. For example, there could be seven payments, the first made after the foundation is laid, the last after the time for all mechanic's liens has run out. (See Chapter 2.) A home renovation loan will often incorporate many of the features of a construction loan. Generally speaking, if you can get all the money up front (or at least at your disposal), it makes it a lot easier to control the contractor and the project.

Is there a problem with my credit?   ☐ yes   ☐ no

If you know of a problem you have with your credit, it would do you well to fix it, if at all possible, before you apply for financing for your renovation project. If you are unaware of a problem, but aren't sure, then applying for your own credit report is probably a good idea. The cost is minimal (typically under $10 a report); you should apply to each of the three national credit report bureaus: Experian (800-397-3742—*www.experian.com*), Trans Union (800-888-4213—*www.tuc.com*), and Equifax (800-685-1111—*www.Equifax.com*). Each specializes in a different geographical area of the country, but lenders often contact all three. Check over your credit report carefully.

Can I fix my credit problem?   ☐ yes   ☐ no

Many credit problems are errors. Your social security number, name, or address may be wrong in the credit report. A lender may be reporting a late payment or loan default when it actually belongs on someone else's account. Check with the bureaus listed above for the exact means for correcting errors. Most can be fixed simply by providing the correct or updated information. On the other hand, actual late payments, defaults, foreclosures, and bankruptcies cannot be fixed. These will continue on your report for many years and can adversely affect your credit. The best you are likely to accomplish is to include an explanatory statement. For example, you were out of work and couldn't pay your bills. But you've been working steadily for the past four years and have consistently paid all your bills. It's not as good as a clean report, but with lenders eager to loan money these days, it may be good enough.

Have I been preapproved?

☐ yes   ☐ no

The preapproval process is now standard with almost all lenders. It's used for all major refinances. Basically, what it amounts to is your applying for financing typically through a mortgage broker, bank, or other lender. You fill out an extensive application, your credit history is checked, for large loans your employment status and bank deposits are checked, and then the lender issues a commitment. It will offer you up to a certain amount of money based on what it says your maximum affordable monthly payment is. Usually, most people are very pleased to learn how much they can borrow. Of course, be careful . . . borrow only as much as you need, not necessarily as much as the lender wants to loan you.

How soon should I borrow the money?

☐ yes   ☐ no

It depends on the type of financing you are getting. If you have applied for and will receive a revolving line of credit through a home equity loan, then don't borrow the money until you actually need it to make a payment to the contractor or the materials supplier. Since you're only charged interest on the amount you borrow from the date that you borrow, wait as long as possible. On the other hand, if you have a single lump-sum financing, through a new first mortgage, then you will probably want to conclude the financing before you begin any construction. (Indeed, you may find that you won't be able to get financing if you begin work because of complications from mechanic's lien procedures. See Chapter 2 for information on mechanic's liens.)

How much should I borrow?

☐ yes   ☐ no

The rule with financing is to get all that you need the first time. If you guess wrong and need more later on, you will find that it's harder to get additional money. If you're getting a revolving line of credit, get it for substantially more than you anticipate you'll need. Since you're not charged until you actually borrow the money, nothing will go to waste. And if you need additional funds, they will be available. If you're getting a lump sum, you'll want to cut it as close as possible, since you won't want to be paying interest on borrowed money that you don't need. Even here, however, it's probably wise to get more than you anticipate you'll need. Remember, with renovation it almost always costs more than you think it will.

Will the interest be tax deductible?   ☐ yes   ☐ no

Generally speaking, the interest on a mortgage up to one million dollars may be tax deductible, if the money is used to purchase a home. On a secondary refinancing, the interest on the mortgage up to $100,000 may be tax deductible. Special rules may apply particularly where the money is used for renovation work. You should check with your accountant to be sure in your case.

Questions to Ask Your Lender

What is the maximum amount you will lend?   ☐ yes   ☐ no

It may be more than you need; it could be less. However, it's important to know the maximum, just in case you find that the renovation project is going to cost you more than you at first anticipated. (Remember the old maxim? Add up the high, the low, and the middle bids to come up with the true cost!)

What is the lowest interest-rate/length-of-loan combination?   ☐ yes   ☐ no

This is very tricky. Listen carefully. You'll quickly find that comparing loans is like comparing apples and twigs. Each has its own parameters. However, every loan will have three things in common: the interest rate, the term (length), and these two together will determine the monthly payment. Sometimes it's worthwhile to get a slightly higher monthly payment if you can pay off the loan earlier. For example, you can often get a lender to cut one point in the interest rate *if* you're willing to accept a 15-year loan as opposed to a 30-year loan. The same may be true for shorter-term financing.

What are the closing costs?

☐ yes ☐ no

The lender should be very specific on these and should provide you with several statements detailing the costs. Keep in mind that any time you put a new mortgage on your property, you're going to have to get title insurance (to cover the lender) and run an escrow (to handle the transaction). Both of these cost money. In addition, the lender will have all sorts of fees. Make a determined effort to find out what these are up front. It may turn out that the lender who offers the lowest interest rate has the highest fees, which would make you reconsider the financing. With short-term financing (home equity and home renovation loans) lenders will often blend all of the fees into a slightly higher interest rate. In that case, it will appear there are no closing costs. If you are short of cash, this could be the way to go. However, the slightly higher interest rate will result in a slightly higher payment.

Will I have to pay for an appraisal?

☐ yes ☐ no

The answer is undoubtedly yes, but then ask if the lender will blend it into the slightly higher interest rate (along with other fees). For some home equity loans, where the value of your property is considerably more than the loan amount (you have a very low LTV), ask the lender to accept a "drive by" appraisal. The appraiser simply drives through the neighborhood, then parks across the street from your home and writes up the appraisal without every going inside or examining the property closely. This is possible because real estate values are primarily determined by location. A drive-by appraisal may only be $200. For a full-blown appraisal, expect to pay $250 to $350.

Will I have to pay for a credit report?

☐ yes ☐ no

Sometimes the lender will ask you to pay; other times it may be blended into the loan. Most major lenders can get a credit report for around $25. However, they sometimes will mark that fee up so that if you have to pay for it, it could cost you $50 to $65. At the present time, the federal government is fighting some markups in court.

Are there any other fees of any kind?   ☐ yes   ☐ no

Be sure you get a detailed accounting of the fees. Lenders seem to be able to come up with fees as fast as the imagination can conceive them. This is one reason to get a "no fees" loan where the costs are blended into the interest rate—you don't get nickel and dimed to death by the extra (and often unnecessary) costs. These fees can include: administrative fee, underwriting fee, origination fee, processing fee, mailing fee, attorney fee, courier fee, documentation fee, and so on. All of the above-mentioned costs are usually considered "garbage fees."

What do I have to do to apply?   ☐ yes   ☐ no

The lender will undoubtedly want you to fill out an application and possibly submit some documentation such as pay stubs or tax returns. You may also be asked to pay for a credit report and appraisal up front. Keep in mind that if you put up the money for these and then don't go with this lender, you will probably have lost the money, as you may be asked to come up with it again for a different lender. The point is, make sure you know what you want before you go for it.

How long will it take to fund?   ☐ yes   ☐ no

Expect an answer such as "two weeks to 30 days, if there are no problems." If you have credit issues, these may have to be straightened out before any lender will move forward. Simple problems, such as errors of name, social security number, address, and so on can often be quickly corrected. More complex problems, such an old lender who hasn't removed a loan from your records that you paid off years earlier, can take longer. (You'll probably need to contact the lender and go through the procedures for getting the old loan removed from your credit report.) Bad credit such as late payments, defaults, foreclosures, and bankruptcies may simply prevent you from getting the loan you want. (You will probably be able to get some sort of loan, but it could be at a higher interest rate.) In addition, some lenders will take longer to fund because they don't happen to have the cash available when you need it. Typically, without serious problems, most mortgages can be funded within 30 days.

Will you fund as a lump sum or as a construction loan? ☐ yes ☐ no

Find out the lender's policy. If you've tied the loan into the renovation, then some lenders will only offer a construction-type loan where the payments are made in installments. On the other hand, if you have a refinance, there may be one lump-sum payment. There could even be a revolving line of credit. Determine what you want, and then see how flexible the lender can be. You may find that with an inflexible lender, you will want to borrow your money elsewhere. It's best to find this out early before you're too committed.

Will the loan be a second mortgage on my property? ☐ yes ☐ no

If you already have a first mortgage on your property that you are not refinancing, then the new loan will probably be a second mortgage. Exceptions could be if you have an existing first and second, in which case the new loan will be a third (rare), or if you are getting a noncollateralized loan (very rare). Be sure you know what the lender is giving you. Don't be surprised to learn later that you've refinanced your entire first mortgage when you thought you were getting a small second. (Sometimes this pays if you get an overall lower interest rate.)

Is there a prepayment penalty? ☐ yes ☐ no

The lender will tell you. Avoid loans with prepayment penalties. This means that if you pay back the loan early (you refinance because rates have dropped), there's a penalty, sometimes amounting to thousands of dollars. These days you can easily get a loan without a prepayment penalty. Indeed, many lenders are offering a quarter point or more discount in their loans *if* you agree to accept a prepayment penalty. My suggestion is that in most cases, you should forego the discount. It won't seem like very much if there's a sudden crisis and you must pay off the loan early, only to find there's thousands of dollars in penalties.

Are payments made directly to me? ☐ yes ☐ no

Your lender may want to make payments to your contractor. This is distinctly to your disadvantage, as noted in
Chapter 2. Ask the lender, if it won't make payments
directly to you, will it make payments in the form of a
two-party check, where both you and the contractor must
sign? If the lender still refuses and insists on paying contractors and materials suppliers directly, I would look for
another lender. Your loss of control over the project
would be too severe. Note: In some states (such as California) lenders are prohibited from making payments to
the contractor alone.

Questions to Ask Your Attorney

**Are there any clauses in the documents that could
hurt me?** ☐ yes ☐ no

Most people don't take their loan documents to attorneys
to see that the documents are reasonable. This is unfortunate because you can be sure that the lender is using a
battery of attorneys to catch every loophole favoring you,
the borrower! An attorney can look over the loan documents and determine if they are fair-minded or if some
clauses in them are unreasonable. True, an attorney may
cost you a bit, but could save you far more. (On the East
Coast, attorneys are usually available to handle an entire
real estate transaction for around a $1000 or less—their
fees for just checking loan docs should be considerably
lower.) Ask your attorney to list any clauses in the loan
docs that could potentially harm you.

Should I renegotiate or go with a different lender? ☐ yes ☐ no

Your attorney is presumably an unbiased, expert third
party. He or she should be able to give you an opinion as
to whether or not the loan is written so unfavorably as to
make it worth your while to look elsewhere. If that's the
case, then you may want to attempt a renegotiation with

the lender. Don't assume that the lender won't deal. Most lenders are willing to make at least minor changes to their loans, if they legally can, and if the borrower has good reasons to ask for them. You may even want to have your attorney call your lender.

What should I demand be added or removed?   ☐ yes ☐ no

Be very careful here. If you ask your attorney, chances are that he or she will want to delete a whole raft of paragraphs that overly favor the lender and add others that favor you. However, this is not like negotiating over the purchase of a home. I've never seen a lender, at least with home loans, who was willing to allow someone other than its own attorneys to make changes to the loan docs. The chances for creating errors that could cause the lender penalties or could allow you to weasel out of paying are too great. Rather, it's best to ask the attorney for a list of items to be removed and added, then speak to the lenders about making the actual changes.

Should I sign the loan documents?   ☐ yes ☐ no

This is the critical opinion that you're paying the attorney for. If he or she says you should sign, you're probably on pretty safe ground. However, most attorneys I've met couch their advice with lots of caveats: sign *if* it's okay with your financial advisor; sign *if* you feel that it's right for you; sign *if* you can afford it. Or, your lawyer may advise you not to sign. I'd be very wary of any loan docs that an attorney advised me not to sign.

5
Doing It Yourself

Questions to Ask Yourself

Do I want to do all the work myself?   ☐ yes   ☐ no

You may. If you're healthy, strong, and have the heart of a
do-it-yourselfer, you may be up and ready for the chal-
lenge of doing all of the renovation work yourself. (Think
of all the money you'll save!) Here's a word of advice,
however. Even if you intend to do it all yourself, plan as if
you're going to hire it out. Then, if you do end up doing
the work on your own, you can take all that money you
didn't spend on labor and put it in the bank, or take a
great vacation, or whatever. And you can crow to your
friends on how much money you saved. On the other
hand, if it turns out that you've bitten off more than you
can chew, you'll have the money to call in professional
help to take over and finish the job. And you won't feel
quite so foolish.

What about doing some of it myself?   ☐ yes   ☐ no

Doing part of the work is a realistic compromise that
many people opt for. For example, when I do a renovation
these days, I hire out all the "heavy lifting" rough work.
Then I do all the finish work myself. Most contractors are
willing to go along with a plan where they do the work
up to a certain point, get paid, and leave, and then you
take over. Be wary, however, of trying to work side by
side with the contractor. Most won't like it; they want to
be in charge. On the other hand, since it's your house, you
will want to be in charge. It makes for a bad working mar-

riage. If you have special skills, such as handling plumbing, electrical, or plastering, then by all means lead those. But don't get in over your head by attempting to save money in areas where you are inexperienced . . . this may even be somewhat dangerous to yourself and the project!

Will I really save any money by doing it myself? ☐ yes ☐ no

Yes, you will save money if you can do a professional job in a reasonable amount of time. No, you won't save money if you go in there, make a mess, and then have to hire a pro to come in and finish it (read, clean up your mess, and start over). If you can do it right, you can save 50 percent or more on the overall costs, depending on how much you do. If you do the work of a GC (general contractor) and sub out all of the labor to subcontractors, you can save anywhere between 15 and 30 percent. Note that just by acting as a GC and not even touching a hammer, you can still save a considerable amount of money.

Have I asked my contractor if he or she will agree to this? ☐ yes ☐ no

Don't assume that the contractor is going to be thrilled to have you working on the project. Remember, by doing some of the work yourself, you're probably creating a headache for him or her. I can recall telling a contractor that I was planning to do all the plumbing, electrical, and finish work on a second-story remodeling. He hit his head with his hand, sighed, and said, "I'm gone!" And he was. He didn't wait for me to explain that I could handle the work. He just didn't want the hassle. The next contractor, on the other hand, was more agreeable, work went well, and the project came out fine. Ask your contractor and find out just how agreeable to the idea he or she really is.

Do I have time to do the work? ☐ yes ☐ no

It's usually a great mistake to think that you'll do renovation work in your "spare time." In our modern society, few of us have any real spare time. What with work, family, recreation, and commuting, ask yourself just when you will fit in the renovation work. If your answer is, "I'll do it on weekends," forget it. You may be willing to commit a few weekends to the project, but after a month or so, I guarantee that the whole concept will get very old. The rule is that if you can't afford to take time off work to do the renovation, hire a professional. Most people who have successfully renovated anything from a bathroom to a whole house had a block of time—weeks to months— available. If you don't, reconsider doing it yourself (at least doing it entirely on your own).

What will it cost me to do the work myself?

☐ yes   ☐ no

Your time is valuable. If you have to take off work, how much money will you not make during that time? That's the cost to you. If you're planning on doing it on your vacation, how much will it cost in weakened family relationships? (Vacations are important time. Don't just assume that you can spend them hammering and painting and not pay an emotional price.) When you calculate any lost funds and any emotional consequences of working on the project yourself, you may learn that you can't afford to do it yourself!

Do I know how to do the work myself?

☐ yes   ☐ no

This is an entirely different and important question. You can know for sure that you're capable only if you've done it in the past. Don't assume you can handle a renovation project just because you know how to swing a hammer and cut wood with a saw. For example, one of the most important phases of the work is demolition— safely removing the existing portion of the home, yet not removing too much or damaging areas that need to be saved. It's almost more an art than a science. If you haven't handled the demolition involved in renovation, you'll be very surprised to discover how cognitive a skill it is. If this is your first major renovation project, my suggestion is that you pay someone else to do it . . . and watch carefully. Then try your hand at it the second time around.

Am I a good "handyman?"

☐ yes   ☐ no

If you are, it's a good indication that you can handle a renovation project. If, over the years, you've replaced doors and windows, put in water heaters, fixed roofs, patched plumbing, and so forth, you may very well find it challenging and fun to do a major renovation project. On the other hand, if your experience is limited to changing light bulbs and fixing washers, quite frankly, you probably aren't a handyman and aren't suited to doing the work on a major renovation project. One way to tell is to take a look at your workbench. (You have a workbench, don't you?) If it's filled with professional tools that you use regularly, then you probably are a handyman. On the other hand, if it's filled with tools you bought at the drugstore or grocery store and seldom use, then you're probably not. Being realistic may be hard, but better now than after you've spent tons of money and time on a project that's frustrating to you.

Is it really important to me to do the work myself?   ☐ yes   ☐ no

On the other hand, sometimes the desire to do your own project can overcome all sorts of handicaps. Many people want the pleasure of being able to say, "I did it." This can be extremely important to them. If you really want to do the work yourself, but aren't the "handy" sort, then my suggestion is that you hire someone compatible to work with you. This other person, probably a carpenter, can direct the project, and show you what needs to be done and how to do it. And you can do it, or most of it, yourself.

Can I handle the heavy lifting?   ☐ yes   ☐ no

It's important to understand that home renovation projects are much like other types of construction in that they require some heavy lifting. Even a single eight-foot two-by-four can weigh 20 pounds or more if it's fairly green wood. A four-by-eight-foot sheet of five-eighths-inch drywall can weigh 40 to 50 pounds. Sinks, windows, and flooring are heavy. A typical small box of tile is 60 pounds or more. In short, even the lightweight stuff (not talking about heavy beams, cement, or other heavier materials) can be heavy for the average person. If you have weak stomach muscles or a bad back, this is not the sort of thing you should get into. You'll find the hospital bills, or time lost in bed, will not be worth any potential savings on the project.

Do I have any physical limitations that might cause me to get injured? ☐ yes ☐ no

It's important to be honest here. If you have heart or vascular trouble, palsy, or anything at all that can prevent you from doing unrestricted physical activity, you should reconsider doing all or even any of the work yourself. Remember, construction work by its very nature can be dangerous. Beams can fall, flooring can break, and someone else can turn a board around accidentally aimed your way. There's always dirt and dust on the site. You need to be alert and able to dodge, jump, and handle unclean air. In short, you need to be physically fit to do the work. If for any reason you're not, leave it to others who are.

Can I handle an electric saw and drill? ☐ yes ☐ no

The answer should be a confident, "yes." Not, "I can learn." Maybe you can learn. And maybe you can't. I've seen too many novices out there who've lost a finger because they haven't had years of experience handling electric tools. If you've been doing it off and on since you were a kid, then it's very likely that you're going to be able to handle the heavyweight tools that construction requires. On the other hand, if this is all new to you, keep in mind that the learning curve is steep. Yes, anyone can turn on a saw and start a wood cut. But what to do instantly when the blade binds or the saw jumps takes experience.

What about a hammer, level, and square? ☐ yes ☐ no

Anyone can hammer, right? Absolutely, but can you get the nail in straight . . . without hammering your finger? As noted previously, if you've been doing it for years, this will seem simpleminded. But most people haven't grown up that way. Most people haven't had the need to do heavy construction work. My suggestion is that you try this out. Get a couple of two-by-fours and nail them together in half a dozen places. Easy? Then you're all set. On the other hand, if you've got bent nails and your arm hurts, it's a sign that you should be an observer.

Do I really know plumbing? ☐ yes ☐ no

If you're new to renovation work, you'll quickly discover that the really expensive areas include plumbing and electrical work. Professionals in these areas get, and deserve, very high pay. Thus, if you can do some of their work yourself, you can save a lot of money. The question is, can you? The answer is, you probably can, if you're willing to study the subject. It's surprising to many, but plumbing is largely a cognitive skill. Figuring out where to put drains and vents and what size and type of pipe to use is very tricky and requires a lot of knowledge and skill, some of which you can learn from books. As far as the physical aspect is concerned, if you can cut, glue, and solder pipe (again all learnable), you can probably do the job. Of course, lifting heavy sinks, tubs, and toilets into place is not easy and not for everyone, but for most people who are willing, it is doable. Note: have a professional do any work with gas. It's not worth the liability to do it yourself. And have a professional inspect all your work.

Do I really know electrical work? ☐ yes ☐ no

As with plumbing, electrical work is a learnable skill. In some respects it's actually easier, since snaking wiring through walls doesn't present nearly the problems that inflexible pipes do. The big concern, of course, is that if you do this wrong it won't just leak, it might burn down the house! Therefore, I suggest that if you want to do it yourself and you're not a professional, you should at the very least have a pro work with you and examine your work to see that it's done correctly. (Don't just rely on a building inspector to catch your mistakes–inspectors are very busy and seldom have time to go over everything.) There are many books available on how to handle electrical wiring, including the excellent series from Sunset. You'll also want to check into a copy of the electrical section of the Uniform Building Code to make sure that your work is up to code. But most importantly, *turn off all electricity* before doing any electrical work. Then, have a professional inspect it before turning the current back on.

Can I make fine cabinetry?   ☐ yes   ☐ no

Many people have a dream about woodworking. They feel
that it's like getting back to basics: the solid, honest, real
things in life. Feeling the wood, working with the grain,
sawing, trimming, sanding . . . there's almost a mystique
about it. Some hope to build fine furniture. For others, it's
creating cabinets as part of a renovation project. I've seen
owners pour money into electric saws, sanders, lathes,
drills, and other specialized woodworking equipment. Of
course, there's nothing wrong with this, as long as you
realize that it's a labor of love. Economically it seldom
makes sense. Usually, you can buy fine cabinets for far less
than you can make them. It's something to consider.

Can I put in finish work?   ☐ yes   ☐ no

Finish work includes painting, putting up moldings, light
switches, faucets—all the things that are done after the
major renovation work is completed. As with electrical
work and plumbing, this is highly detailed work, and if
you do it yourself, you can save a bundle. The problem,
however, is that the finish work is what really shows. Do
it badly, and no matter how well the basic work was
done, the overall project will look bad. If you're handy
and are willing to go slowly and do a good job, you
shouldn't have many problems. However, don't expect to
whiz through this and have it come out looking great. As
I said, this is detail work.

Can I do plastering?   ☐ yes   ☐ no

Anybody can slap some plaster on a wall, right? Actually,
these days there is very little plastering done in most construction. Of course, if you use stucco on the outside, you
could do it yourself. But this is a specialized job and
you'd be better off calling in a professional, at least if you
want it to look good. Inside it's mostly drywall, which is
taped, and then a texture applied typically with a spray
gun. Yes, you can rent the equipment and do it yourself.
But again, considering the learning curve, it's probably
cheaper to have a pro do the whole thing for you.

Have I had any previous successes or failures?   ☐ **yes**   ☐ **no**

This is important–if you've done home renovation projects in the past and been successful, you can build on
those successes to feel confident doing even more ambi-
tious projects. Success leads to success in this area. On the
other hand, if things didn't turn out right, if it didn't look
good, if you had to call someone else in to finish the job,
don't think that this time it will be different; listen to what
your previous experience is telling you. You may be an
excellent accountant, teacher, retailer, entrepreneur, or
whatever, but perhaps construction work just isn't your
forte. You may want to do it to save money, for the exercise, or just for the bragging rights. But in reality, not
doing it could be the better decision.

Do I believe that I'll do as good a job as professionals?   ☐ **yes**   ☐ **no**

This is the ultimate question you have to answer. You
may be perfectly capable of getting the job done. But
results count. How good will it look? If it ends up looking
amateurish, it will detract from the home; when you sell
your home, a bad renovation job could even force you to
take less. If you can get in there and produce professional
results, then by all means do it. It you can't, leave it to a
pro.

Questions to Ask Your Spouse (or Significant Other)

Are you willing to let me spend time working on the   ☐ **yes**   ☐ **no**
project?

I had a friend who was determined to put an addition onto
his house by himself. He worked every weekend and
evenings for seven months, and when he was done, he had
accomplished two things: a beautiful renovation . . . and a
divorce. If you're going to do it yourself, be sure that your
spouse or significant other understands what's involved in

terms of time and commitment, and signs off on it. If both of you work on the project together, that's even better. But if your spouse or significant other sees the project as taking time and energy away from your relationship, you could be headed for big emotional trouble. By putting what's involved on the table, you can determine before you start what the toll will be. And perhaps, to save a relationship, you might decide that even though you could do it yourself, you should hire someone else.

Will you support me when the going gets rough?   ☐ yes   ☐ no

You have to get an honest answer. Sometimes, to please you, your spouse or significant other will initially agree to go along with the project. But then, you're busy all the time, and you won't go out to dinner, dancing, or a ball game. You're too tired afterward to give much attention to him or her. Add to this mix possible financial difficulties due to your misjudging how much the project will cost. Or perhaps you've injured yourself and now need to be cared for. When things get really rough in the trenches, will your spouse or significant other still be willing to support you and the project? It's something to consider.

Will you be satisfied if it turns out looking less than professional?   ☐ yes   ☐ no

My wife always supports me when I do a renovation project. However, she's extremely critical of the final product. If it doesn't look 100-percent professional, she'll tell me . . . and insist that I do something about it, even if that means calling in a pro to take out my work and do it right! (That actually happened once, a long time ago!) Remember, you probably can't get away with just satisfying yourself. (We all tend to be very forgiving when it comes to our own work.) You'll need to satisfy others. If you're worried about doing that, it's a definite warning flag. On the other hand, if you're positive that others will see your work in a good light, then by all means, proceed full speed ahead!

How long have I got before I give up and demand that someone else come in and do it?

☐ yes   ☐ no

None of us has unlimited time. Recently the electric plugs in my kitchen went out. After I turned off the power, I began tracing down the problem. The circuit breaker was fine. The circuit itself was fine. Everything seemed perfect, except that the plugs didn't work. After two days of not being able to use appliances in the kitchen, my wife threw up her hands and said, "Call an electrician!" I had used up all my time. You may find that you only have so much time, too. It might be best if you got this out into the open before you begin the project. If you only have a month and it's going to take six to do it, once again you might want to reconsider doing it yourself. In my case, I persevered. With the help of a continuity tester, I discovered that a rodent had chewed through a wire in a wall. I subsequently cut into walls, replaced the wire, and fixed the mess. All was forgiven. Maybe I was lucky.

6
Bath, Bed, and Kitchen Decisions

Questions to Ask Yourself About Your Bathroom

Will more than one person be using the bathroom? ☐ yes ☐ no

This is particularly important with the bath next to the master bedroom. If a couple gets up for work at the same time and both want to brush their teeth, you'd better have a bathroom with two sinks. Similarly, the toilet and the shower should be separated, preferably with the toilet in its own cubicle. That's the way it's done in most new upscale homes. Why should your home be any less?

Do I need an additional bathroom? ☐ yes ☐ no

If your home only has one bathroom, the answer is an immediate yes. These days, two baths are minimal, even if one is only a toilet and a sink. If you have two, then it's a matter of how upscale you want to go and how much money you can afford to spend. In palatial homes, there's one bathroom for each bedroom plus an additional bath for guests, on each floor. If that's a bit excessive, then consider a fine home. Most people seem to need three bathrooms as minimal—one for the master bedroom, one for the other bedrooms, and one as a bathroom for guests when entertaining. Adding bathrooms definitely will add to the elegance of any home.

Is the water pressure high enough in the shower or tub? ☐ yes   ☐ no

There's nothing more annoying than trying to take a shower where the water pressure is inadequate. You can never seem to get your hair clean of shampoo. Usually this happens in older homes. Buy a pressure gauge (they only cost about $20) and check the water pressure outside in front of your home. 40 to 70 psi is usually considered normal. If it's less, you may want to talk to your water company about increasing it. If it's normal, and you still have trouble with your shower, then chances are it's not the pressure, but the flow that's to blame. Chances are you have old pipes that are corroded and blocking the flow. The easiest solution may be to have a plumber run a new cold line from outside the house, where the pressure is normal, right to the new shower or tub you're installing, and another hot line directly from your water heater. That way you'll be able to enjoy a warm shower with lots of water pressure.

Is there enough hot water for showers and baths? ☐ yes   ☐ no

A separate issue is whether there is enough hot water for all of the showers and baths that your family may take. Today a minimum-sized water heater for a family is considered to be 50 gallons. Forty years ago the minimum size was only 30 gallons. If you have an older house, your water heater may simply be too small. Consider updating to a larger heater. By the way, the new heater should be so much more efficient that you won't notice an increase in your utility bills! Note that sometimes a large water heater will not produce much hot water because it has filled with silt. Try draining the tank using the spigot at the bottom (and a hose leading the water safely outside). If you get grit coming out of the end, it may be time to install a new heater, even if the old one isn't leaking.

Does my current bathroom have enough countertop area? ☐ yes   ☐ no

This is particularly a problem in small bathrooms. In your existing bathroom, do you have room to put brushes,

shaving paraphernalia, hair blowers, curlers, and flatten-
ers, plus the other items that you may want to keep handy
in your bathroom? If not, then you'll want to redesign the
new bathroom with more countertop area. This is possible, if you're creative, even without increasing the size of
the bathroom. It's a matter of utilizing the area you have
better. For example, sometimes it's possible to extend
some countertop area over a toilet, or next to a tub or
shower. Of course, if your budget allows it, and you can
find the area to expand into, by all means consider increasing the size of your bathroom. It will only make it look
more elegant and be more functional.

Is there enough storage space in my current bathroom? ☐ yes ☐ no

Of one thing you can be sure—you can't have too much
storage space. In bathrooms there are typically only two
storage areas: in the cabinet beneath the sink and in the
medicine cabinet. If this is inadequate, you may want to
increase the amount of cabinet space. Be creative. You may
be able to sink a cabinet into a wall that has a closet behind
it. This would give you more storage area, without taking
up more floor space. Or consider floor-to-ceiling racks for
storage. Some are quite attractive. If this is your problem,
address it, or else you'll be as unhappy with the new bathroom as you are with the old.

Do I have a water-saving toilet? ☐ yes ☐ no

The amount of water that a toilet uses is measured in
either gallons or liters per flush. Modern toilets use very
little water, in the range of a single gallon. Older toilets
frequently use three to five gallons of water. If you currently have an older, less-efficient toilet, you may want
to consider switching to one of the newer water-saving
models. In addition to conserving water, which is something important to do almost anywhere you live in the
country today, the efficiency of modern toilets allows for
many new designs including "lo-boy" and "tankless."
Check around. Buying a new toilet may not only cut
down on your water bill, but may also spruce up your
bathroom.

Does my bathroom need more light?

☐ yes ☐ no

Consider the plight of the architect trying to design an efficient house. Every room needs light, and lots of it. So the architect tries to put the most important rooms at the periphery of the house where they have the most open exposure. Bedrooms, the kitchen, dining room, and living room all need outside windows. And what does that leave? It leaves very little room for the lowly bathroom, which often gets stuck with a tiny outside window or none at all. If your current bathroom is suffering in this way, consider adding more light. While redesigning the house to give the bathroom more outside access is not really a good idea, there are three options. Increase the existing window size, add more artificial light, or add a skylight.

Do I want carpeting in my new bathroom?

☐ yes ☐ no

To some this speaks of elegance. To others it seems absurd. Regardless of your perspective, take a moment to consider this as a possibility. Wall-to-wall carpeting in a bathroom is warm and comfortable underfoot, it is relatively easy to keep clean, and it costs a fraction of what a tile or stone floor costs. Throw rugs in critical areas can be removed for washing. If you're set on Italian tiles, then by all means go forward with that plan. But if you're on a budget, this is something that may become increasingly interesting to you.

Do I want tile in my new bathroom?

☐ yes ☐ no

Historically, tile has always been a bathroom favorite going back to the ancient Romans. It washes easily, looks very good (even elegant), and the smaller tiles can be fairly easily installed. However, bathroom tile does have its downside. The grout can become dirty and contaminated. It can be slippery, unless covered with a rubber-backed throw rug. And if you fall, it's a very hard surface to land upon. If you're considering tile for your bathroom, consider some of the nonskid surfaces for the floor. And consider a very narrow grout line, so there's less room for dirt and bacteria to grow. Oh, and wash it often.

Do I want marble or granite in my new bathroom?   ☐ yes   ☐ no

Either is wonderful for floor, countertop, and backsplash. While marble is too soft for kitchen counters, the much lower usage makes it a much better candidate for a bathroom. If you elect to use stone in your bathroom, you'll be not only making a fashion statement, but a price statement as well. These are probably the most expensive surfaces you can use . . . and most people know it. Do you want your bathroom to look expensive? Use marble and granite, and you're guaranteed that it will. Note that recently using a combination of granite for the countertop, marble for the floor, and tile for the walls in complementing colors and styles has become very fashionable for the most elegant of homes.

Do I want a particular style in my new bathroom?   ☐ yes   ☐ no

Unlike with kitchens, where what you have is often what you get, with bathrooms there is the opportunity to create a theme. It could be Arabian Nights, or ultramodern, or early American, or whatever. But by the prudent use of tiles, woods, and other materials, you can transform a previously bland bathroom into a stylish period piece. And don't overlook the use of faux paint and wallpaper for the walls to complete the effect.

How much am I willing to spend?   ☐ yes   ☐ no

Of course, this is the ultimate question. You can create all sorts of styles and designs, but what it really boils down to is what you can afford. Here are a couple of helpful hints. You don't necessarily have to do all of your renovation at once. By breaking it up into years, you may be able to do a bigger, better, and more expensive job. Perhaps this is the year of the bathroom. Next year it's the year of the kitchen. Another alternative is to bang your budget. Steal from other areas (such as a bedroom) to create a better bathroom. Perhaps you'll even reduce the extent of your renovation in order to make the bathroom better. And then, of course, there's always the alternative of just spending more!

Questions to Ask Yourself About Your Bedroom

Is it spacious enough?   ☐ yes   ☐ no

Newer homes tend to have huge bedrooms, mainly because builders recognize this as a feature that buyers crave. However, if your house is older, chances are the bedroom is quite small. Indeed, it may not even have a master bathroom off of it, which is considered an absolute necessity in homes today. When renovating an older house, consider adding room to your master bedroom. This can be done by adding on to the house. It can also be done by breaking down a wall between a master bedroom and another bedroom (or closet) and expanding into that space. And while you're at it, add a master bathroom, if you don't already have one.

Do I want to use the bedroom for multiple purposes?   ☐ yes   ☐ no

Bedrooms are for sleeping. And more. The "more" can take many forms. Additional uses include: sitting room, exercise room, study, office, and so on. Of course, this assumes that you have a large master bedroom (see previous section). As part of your renovation, you may want to delineate more clearly a portion of your master bedroom to emphasize its multiple use. For example, you may want to create an alcove near a window that's perfect for a reading area. A nook to one side could be ideal for a treadmill. If you don't have a home with enough separate space for all of these uses to have their own rooms, then consider portioning off a part of the master bedroom. Chances are, much of the excess space in the bedroom goes to waste anyhow.

Does it have enough closet space?   ☐ yes   ☐ no

No one has enough closet space. Even if you start out with too much closet space, you'll end up with too little. It's a rule that our "stuff" expands to fill all the available room, and more. Therefore, if you're renovating any bedroom in the house, consider putting in more closet space. Of course, adding on to the basic plan for closets is an enormously expensive way to go. However, you can sometimes expand a closet into a part of the garage that's unused, or perhaps a utility room that's underutilized. Always consider the closet option.

Are the windows adequate?   ☐ yes   ☐ no

Most modern homes, regardless of the climate, include double-pane windows. This provides two benefits. It cuts down the cost of heating and cooling and makes the room more comfortable to be in. And it reduces noise from the outside. If your existing master or other bedroom has old-fashioned steel or aluminum single-pane windows, consider replacing them with modern plastic or wood and metal double-pane windows. The cost is about $350 for a modest-sized window, not including installation, and goes up from there. There are many companies, such as Milgard, that will build windows to fit. They can be retrofitted simply by removing the existing windowpanes and screwing the new windows in. Also consider getting low-e (emissivity) windows, which reduces radiant heat loss and gain.

Does it need a ceiling fan?   ☐ yes   ☐ no

Regardless of how well insulated a bedroom is, or how good the heating and cooling systems are, an overhead fan is an asset. It helps to stir the air around in the summer, making you feel cooler. And it can circulate the air in the winter, helping to warm the room. Besides, a stylish fan (such as those from Casablanca or Hunter) can add a new dimension to a bedroom. If you do nothing else as part of your bedroom renovation, adding a fan can make a big difference. By the way, be sure to get one with a remote control. It makes it so much easier both to install and later to control the fan's direction and speed.

Will I want carpeting or another type of flooring?   ☐ yes   ☐ no

Wall-to-wall carpeting is considered standard in most bedrooms. Hardwood flooring is considered elegant. If you opt for hardwood, however, you'll then need to add some sort of throw rug carpeting on top. A good oriental rug can easily run into many thousands of dollars, so wall-to-wall carpeting is usually the option of choice for the budget conscious. For those who want to have their cake and eat it too, you might consider hardwood around the periphery of the room. In the center, heavy padding can be put onto a subfloor, and a carpet placed on that. Thus, the carpeting is on very little of the hardwood, meaning that you now only have to pay for one floor. It's cheaper, but has a very stylish appearance.

Should I add a skylight?   ☐ yes   ☐ no

Consider this a possibility if the room is dark and there is no other easier method of lighting it. If the room has a high ceiling, it may be possible to put small windows near the ceiling on an exterior wall to let in light. Adding sconces and light fixtures can also help. If you do add a skylight, keep in mind the noise factor. Rain falling on a skylight can be noisy, much more so than when it falls on a roof with insulation and perhaps attic space beneath. Yes, you may get the extra light. But you may also get sleepless nights during the rainy season.

What would I like for wall and window treatments?   ☐ yes   ☐ no

Elaborate wall coverings and window treatments are the rage these days. There are all sorts of wallpapers available and faux painting (where a paint/glaze solution is dabbed on the walls with a rag or sponge for a textured effect) is well accepted. The windows can be covered with curtains, shades, shutters, blinds, and even draped cloths! If you decide early on as to what wall and window treatments you want, you may be able to cut down on other bedroom expenses such as lighting and carpeting. Often, the style of the room may end up being darker, depending on the treatments chosen.

How much am I willing to spend?   ☐ yes   ☐ no

As always, this is the critical question. If you're on a strict budget, the answer will be "as little as possible," particularly if you're going to need to conserve money to spend on the kitchen and bath. Nevertheless, the bedrooms, particularly the master, are an important part of the home

and not a place to skimp. Remember, it's where you'll
spend a third of your life, so make it as lively as you can
possibly afford.

Questions to Ask Yourself About Your Kitchen

Does the family regularly meet in the kitchen?   ☐ yes   ☐ no

The kitchen can be the "meeting place" for the home.
Often, family business and sometimes work is conducted
on the kitchen table. In some families, it's where the kids
do their homework, where mom or dad sort and follow
recipes, and where everyone gets together when there's
something important to be said or done. If this is the way
that your family operates, then you should consider keeping a large kitchen or expanding a smaller one. You may
want to keep countertop space to a minimum and increase
spot lighting. It's important when renovating that you do
the work that needs to be done, even if it happens to be the
most expensive. If your kitchen is the center of your home,
then you're justified in spending the most money in making it the largest, most important room.

Do you eat in the kitchen?   ☐ yes   ☐ no

Some people eat in the kitchen. Others only prepare food
there and eat more formally in a dining room. And yet
others never eat at home at all! If you eat in your kitchen
on a regular basis, you'll want to include space for this.
How many people eat there regularly? Can you get by
with a high countertop and a few platform chairs? If the
whole family eats at once, you may need a nook where a
table and four to six chairs will fit. When renovating a
kitchen, you usually have the opportunity of doing some
redesign work. When that happens, be sure to take into
account how many people will regularly eat in the
kitchen, and make room for them.

Do I often prepare meals in the kitchen?

☐ yes   ☐ no

If you regularly prepare meals in a kitchen, then you will want lots of countertop space. You'll also want an efficient oven and stove, probably with more than four burners. And you'll want your cabinets organized so that you can easily get to pots and pans as well as dishes and glasses. Think about the kind of food preparation you do, and what will make it easier, when you're considering the purchase of your countertops and cabinets. It's simply not enough that they look nice. They should also make it easier to do the work that you like to do in your kitchen. For example, if you're left-handed, you'll probably want the dishwasher on the left side of the sink. If you're right-handed, it might be easier on the other side.

Will there be more than one person working in the kitchen?

☐ yes   ☐ no

Sometimes both spouses are into gourmet cooking. When it comes time for dinner, there isn't one cook, but two . . . or more! If this is the case with your family, then you may want to think of your kitchen in terms of separate cooking stations. It's not beyond imagination to have two sinks and two stoves in one kitchen! More likely, however, is the use of cooking "triangles." Here, each station is a triangle. For example, the oven, stove, and microwave might be together in one cooking station triangle. The sink, dishwasher, and countertop space make for a cleanup triangle. The oven, breadboard, and cabinet storage make for a baking triangle.

Do I buy a lot of food at once?

☐ yes   ☐ no

Some people buy their food for preparation each day. Others, particularly those with large families, buy their food once a week or even just a couple of times a month. If you buy your food in bulk quantities, you'll want your kitchen to contain extra storage space. This can be built into the kitchen in the form of a pantry. Or if there's not enough room for a pantry, you may want to consider putting in extra cabinets. Room for an extra refrigerator or freezer may also be something you'll want to budget for.

What appliances do I want in my kitchen?   ☐ **yes**   ☐ **no**

Obviously, every kitchen needs a stove, oven, sink, and refrigerator. A garbage disposal and a dishwasher are now considered almost a necessity in all but the most budget-minded of homes. But what about a trash compactor, towel warmer, instant hot water delivery system, or built-in microwave? Would you like or need built-in countertop items such as a blender and can opener? Before you actually get started with your renovation, you may want to create a list of all the appliances you'd like to have in your kitchen, and then design the space, cabinets, and countertop to fit your list.

Does the current traffic flow work?   ☐ **yes**   ☐ **no**

Some kitchens just seem to flow, while others seem to back up. Take a look at the traffic flow in your kitchen. While it's not likely that you'll be able to change the kitchen's location in your home, you might be able to change the flow. If it's awkward getting to a dining room from the kitchen, you might want to put a door through a wall to gain more access. If kids are always tracking mud into the kitchen coming in from outside, perhaps a separate entrance through the garage (with a wash basin nearby) would be helpful. When you're renovating try to be creative. Yes, many traffic-flow features are going to be locked in simply because of the way your home is designed. On the other hand, many times a simple change of wall or doorway can dramatically improve the flow.

Is my current kitchen safe and efficient?   ☐ **yes**   ☐ **no**

Does your oven door open into a walkway so that people are constantly banging into it when they go by? Do you have to walk some distance from your sink to get to the dishwasher? Is the countertop too high for the kids, so they are always scrambling to climb on top of it? Many kitchens are both inefficient and unsafe. Take a close look at the one you've got. Look at it from the perspective of yourself working in it, of children, of others who may be in the kitchen. Do you have a hanging microwave whose door bangs into your head whenever you open it? Make those changes that will create a safer and more efficient kitchen.

Have I made a list of what works in my kitchen? ☐ yes ☐ no

Chances are there are many things that you like about your current kitchen. You may be very pleased about the view from the window in front of the sink. You may like how easy it is to load the dishwasher. And then how simple it is to take the dishes out and put them on shelves. You may like the way the countertop doubles as a snack bar for the kids. You may like the fact that you don't need to stoop over to get to the oven. There are undoubtedly lots of features of your kitchen that you find terrific. Now, before you begin your renovation, make a list of all the features you like. Then you can be sure to retain them in your new kitchen.

Have I made a list of what doesn't work? ☐ yes ☐ no

Similarly, there may be many things about your kitchen that simply don't work. Every time you try to unload dishes you may bang your shin on the dishwasher door. The switch to turn on the garbage disposal may be in an awkward location or in one that's difficult to reach. There may not be enough lighting. The floors may be slippery, causing occasional falls. Just as with the positives, before you start your renovation, make a list of the negative features of your kitchen, those things that don't work for you. Then be sure to take each of those features that don't work out of the new kitchen you create.

Will I have children in the kitchen? ☐ yes ☐ no

If you have small children, then you might have special kitchen needs. Locking cabinets may be a necessity. These can be retrofitted to old cabinets, but some manufacturers include these locks with new models. Similarly, you may want a lock on the stove and dishwasher doors. Some manufacturers include children's locks on these appliances. You may also want to create some countertop area that's lower than standard height, so the kids can use it to prepare snacks, drinks, and even eat food. Perhaps space and connections for a TV would be in order. What about a surface to accommodate a computer that the kids can use? Planning for the use to which you'll put your kitchen can make it far more useful later on.

Does my kitchen need more light?   ☐ yes   ☐ no

What kitchen doesn't? In the past, fluorescent lighting, sometimes hidden in wells in the ceiling, was the lighting of choice. Other times, incandescent fixtures attached to the ceilings were used. However, with the new modern kitchen you create, you can use recessed lighting to highlight all of the areas on the countertop and the area where you'll eat. You can still use fluorescent lighting, of course, but many people object to the green tint it gives everything, especially food. So today, you may not need it. You may even want to cut a new window or skylight to bring in the light of the sun. Think lighting when you're designing your kitchen. It's really much too late to begin thinking about it after all the work has nearly been completed.

Do I need more countertop space?   ☐ yes   ☐ no

You probably do if you're into food preparation in a big way. You also probably need it if you put a lot of things on the countertop such as a popcorn popper, toaster, can opener, microwave, knife set, wine rack, and so on. Consider creating more countertop space by building an island in the center of the kitchen. You can use it for food preparation, for cooking (if you include a stove with it), and for cleanup (if it includes a sink). Think about all of the things you could do with more countertop space. Then think creatively about where you can get it. (One person I knew actually put a refrigerator in her pantry in order to increase the countertop space in a small kitchen. And it worked fine!)

Do I need a bigger oven and stove?   ☐ yes   ☐ no

If your family eats out most of the time, you have to question why you would need a big oven and stove. Indeed, some people don't even use their oven over the course of an average year. Therefore, it may be the case that an average-sized oven and stove will do just fine. (You don't want to put in an undersized unit, as that might make your house less sellable later on.) On the other hand, if you love to bake and cook, then a bigger oven and stove will be very rewarding to you. Be sure that when they are installed, they are perfectly level. It makes a huge difference when baking and frying.

What about a bigger refrigerator?

☐ **yes**   ☐ **no**

The thing about refrigerators is that they take up a lot of room. I'm sure that everyone can use a bigger refrigerator no matter how big his or her current model is. However, keep in mind that if you jump from an 18-cubic-foot to a 30-cubic-foot model, that's a lot of countertop and cabinet space that you'll use up. And unless you're able to sink the refrigerator into the wall, that's a lot of protrusion into the kitchen. The goal is to determine what size refrigerator is right for your family and not get one that's too big . . . or too small.

How much am I willing to spend?

☐ **yes**   ☐ **no**

It's kind of fun to come up with a figure in your mind that covers what you're willing to spend on your kitchen. Then watch that figure grow as you educate yourself as to what's available and how much it costs. I've seen homeowners say things such as, "I'll spend $10,000 on this kitchen," and then spend $50,000 without blinking an eye. Of course, you don't want to overbuild for your home and neighborhood. And you don't want to get over your head into debt. A good course of action is to determine not how much you're willing to, but how much you can justify (in terms of added value and monthly payments) spending in renovating your kitchen. Just keep a flexible attitude. Remember, when it comes to remodeling, everything costs more than you anticipate.

7
Installing Cabinets

Questions to Ask Yourself

Have I checked out new cabinets at building supply stores?

☐ yes ☐ no

Today cabinets are sold at a variety of places. Probably the most easily accessible are building supply stores such as Home Depot, Lowes, and others. Many of these stores offer displays, cabinets set up in mock kitchens and baths so you can see just how they'll look. Such stores often carry cabinets from half a dozen manufacturers, and they can quote prices and handle installation. Indeed, for a nominal fee these stores will often do a three-dimensional virtual layout of your kitchen or bath showing how the cabinets will look in place. You can see what your cabinets might look like before you buy them! Keep in mind, however, that these might not necessarily be the most competitive prices. Be sure to shop around.

Have I called cabinet builders?

☐ yes ☐ no

Most communities have cabinet builders. These are fine woodworkers who produce cabinets from scratch. They tend to be more expensive, but as the old saying goes, you get what you pay for. Here the cabinets are built to fit your kitchen or bath. You can usually get a salesperson to come out and do a diagram of your kitchen. Then he or she will prepare a layout showing where the cabinets will go. The drawback here is that most individual cabinet-makers are very restricted in the styles and woods they offer. You may get good work, but a small selection.

Have I looked for cabinets on the Internet or in magazines? ☐ **yes** ☐ **no**

There are hundreds of quality cabinet manufacturers across the country that advertise both on the Internet and in home magazines. You can often order your cabinets direct from them, or they will direct you to a local dealer. (They also are frequently the same manufacturers who have displays at building supply stores noted previously; find out if they do, and that way you can check out their products in person.) Many of these, such as KraftMaid, WoodMode, and Omega, though not necessarily the biggest, will offer extensive picture galleries and sometimes virtual tours so that you can see what their products look like. Don't overlook this excellent source for cabinet information.

Have I added in the cost of installation? ☐ **yes** ☐ **no**

Keep in mind that cabinets are typically priced sans installation. The cost of putting them in is extra. And when you buy direct from a distant company, they usually do not offer any installation—that's up to you to supply. (Local building supply stores usually *do* offer installation, but often only on the products they sell.) Be sure that you contact a contractor (see following section) about how much it will cost to have the cabinets installed. The price range can be enormous, from only a few hundred dollars to many thousands.

Should I install the cabinets myself? ☐ **yes** ☐ **no**

You can, and many homeowners do. It doesn't require highly technical skills. However, it is finish work, which means that you must often find ways to fill gaps and make things fit that don't want to. In other words, it's up to the installer to make it all come out looking good. Keep in mind that cabinets are big, bulky, and sometimes heavy. You will probably need an additional person to help you. Also, the securing of cabinets to walls, floors, ceilings, and each other can require special fasteners. If you're unfamiliar with cabinet installation, be sure that you learn how to do it before you make the attempt.

Have I created a price comparison list?   ☐ yes   ☐ no

This is very important from a budgeting perspective.
What you will quickly find is that the selection is enormous . . . and hard to track. It will be made easier if you
write out a list comparing styles, colors, features, installation, and price. You could be surprised to find that
cabinets that you thought were unaffordable, when installation and hardware are thrown in, are priced favorably with cabinets that you thought were far less
expensive, and less desirable.

Do I know the maximum price I am willing to pay   ☐ yes   ☐ no
for new cabinets?

Do you have a maximum price you're willing to pay
for new cabinets? Can you stick to it? Often this is part
of a budget established for an entire kitchen or bath
renovation—so much for countertops, appliances, fixtures, and . . . cabinets. Of one thing you can be sure;
you will find cabinets that you dearly love that far and
away exceed the maximum price you have budgeted for
them. You will be sorely tempted to spend more to get
better. Just keep in mind, however, that the bane of
home renovation is upgrading. Chances are you will not
only want better cabinets, but also better everything
else. And if you act on this, your budget will be out the
window. It's a rare home renovator who makes a budget
and can stick to it.

Are the cabinets readily available?   ☐ yes   ☐ no

Availability is an important factor that is frequently over-
looked. You may find the perfect cabinets for you both in
appearance and price, but they may not be available in
the time frame you need. Local cabinetmakers are often
backed up for months. Manufacturers who distribute
nationally may have most pieces in stock, but may be out
one or two crucial units. For example, they may not have
a kitchen sink cabinet, or a corner unit available, even
though all the other pieces you want are ready. You could
be told that you'll have to wait six weeks or more before
they can be sent to you. This can also be the case with

building supply stores, although they are far more likely to offer standard cabinets that are almost always available. Be sure to check availability.

Is there an additional cost for shipping?

☐ yes ☐ no

Freight is typically not included when you buy directly from the manufacturer. However, it is often less than you might suppose, given the size of cabinets. Cabinets are shipped cross-country by rail and truck, and can usually be delivered (once shipped from the factory) within a couple of weeks. The cost may only be a few hundred dollars for all the cabinets in your kitchen or bath. Be sure to check it out and add it to your price comparison sheet.

Have I selected an appropriate wood?

☐ yes ☐ no

You have a large selection of woods to choose from in cabinets. While oak has been the most popular in recent years, other woods from ash to maple are commonly used. Typically cabinets are made from hard wood (which refers to their grain, not necessarily their hardness). Since the availability of hard woods is declining, this tends to boost their prices. As a result, in recent years soft wood cabinets (such as those made of pine) have come into vogue. These are particularly popular in early American styles. If you do opt for these, however, keep in mind that they will tend to dent (get impressions dug into them) more easily than hard woods will.

Are new cabinets the right color and style for my kitchen?

☐ yes ☐ no

Early American, modern, elite—the styles for new cabinets are almost as variable as are the stains and colors available. When you first get started, it may seem as though your choices are endless. However, it's important to temper your selection with common sense. Consider the overall style of your home. Is it New England cottage? Victorian? Mediterranean? Spanish? Colonial? To avoid a clash of styles and colors, it's important that your cabinets, at the least, complement the overall style of your home.

Have I got the correct measurements?   ☐ yes   ☐ no

There's an old rule in construction that goes, "Measure twice, cut once." While you probably won't be doing any cutting here, it certainly won't hurt to measure twice or even three times. This is not usually an issue if you have an installer. However, if you're doing the buying and/or the installing, you'll want to be absolutely sure that your measurements are correct. Cabinet manufacturers will give you precise outside dimensions for their products. It's vitally important that you get the right measurements for your kitchen or bath. Common mistakes include not leaving enough room (or leaving too much) for matching in corners, failing to take into account protruding wall surfaces such as tile, or buying cabinets that are too shallow (or too deep) for the countertop.

Am I leaving the right amount of space for appliances?   ☐ yes   ☐ no

The assumption that many people make is that there is a "standard" size for sinks, ovens, ranges, dishwashers, refrigerators, and so on. While most are within certain boundaries (you're not likely to get a six-foot-wide oven top or a one-foot-wide kitchen sink), there is, nevertheless, great variance. For example, sinks often are anywhere from 30 to 48 inches wide. Their depth may be from 18 to 28 inches. All of which is to say that *before* you buy the cabinets, you should scope out what appliances you are going to be getting. Determine their dimensions to make sure that the holes left for them in the cabinets won't be too large . . . or too small.

Am I getting slide-out shelves?   ☐ yes   ☐ no

These are increasingly popular. Slide-outs are shelves that are on rollers so that when you open the cabinet doors, you can slide them out. It makes it far easier to locate pots, pans, and whatever else you have on the shelves. I encourage you to use slide-out shelves, if possible, on *all* of your kitchen cabinets. You'll notice the difference immediately and every time you use them. They do cost more, but they add so much to the kitchen.

Have I chosen the right hardware?   ☐ yes   ☐ no

While you may not have a choice when it comes to hinges, you often do have a choice with regard to handles. Frequently the manufacturer will include handles that it feels are appropriate to the cabinets. However, you may sometimes choose alternates. Or you may decide simply not to use the handles that come with the cabinets and instead make your own selection. Here's a word of caution, whatever you do. Make sure that the hardware blends well with the overall décor of the cabinets and the kitchen or bath. Bright red porcelain handles do not usually fit with traditional maple cabinets any more than antique bronze handles typically go with ultra modern white cabinets. Think of the overall look rather than a specific effect.

Am I waiting until the appropriate time for installation?   ☐ yes   ☐ no

It may be that the only part of the renovation that you are personally doing is the installation of the cabinets. If that's the case, it's only natural that you will want to get to your job and shine. However, it's important that you temper your enthusiasm with an understanding of work logistics. If your kitchen is being redone, the cabinets are among the last to go in after any structural work, rough plumbing and electrical, insulation, drywall, and in some cases, even painting. If you have the cabinets delivered to the kitchen early, they will be in the way of other workpeople . . . and this could cost you more money in delays. You'll get your chance. Just don't try to get it too soon.

If I'm installing, have I read up on how to do it?   ☐ yes   ☐ no

In today's world of computers and software, it has become common for many people to believe that it's not necessary to read directions. In fact, a common rule is, "If you need to read the instructions, the product is defective!" While that may hold true for high-tech items, keep in mind that cabinets are low-tech. They reach back into antiquity. And often the methods of installation are old and established. All of which is to say that *before* you attempt installation yourself, be sure that you read the manufacturer's instructions. You may be surprised at how simple (or complex) the work is. Be sure to follow the directions carefully, or else your cabinets may not line up, or worse, may become loose or disoriented after your kitchen is finished off. (And then it's too late to do much about it!)

Do I know what I'll do with my old cabinets? ☐ yes   ☐ no

The old cabinets usually come off in sections and may be quite usable. Some people simply have them installed in their garage, where they can provide needed storage space. In other cases, when the old cabinets are in particularly good shape, people will have them stored temporarily in their garage while they attempt to sell them. If you plan on selling your old cabinets, my suggestion is that you do *not* do it until they are removed. If you sell them while they are in place, the buyers will never be happy with them once they are taken out (and slightly banged up in the process). In other cases, they are simply hauled off to the dump. Regardless of what you plan to do, be sure that you have a plan.

For painting cabinets, do I have the right kind of paint? ☐ yes   ☐ no

It is possible to renovate old cabinets by painting them. This is not as hard as it first sounds. Typically, the cabinets must be clean and free of grease. However, contrary to common opinion, you do *not* necessarily have to sand off old paint or stain. Rather, you have to use the correct new paint. To cover cabinets that were previously stained, be sure you use oil-based paint. It will usually seep into the wood and form a strong bond. (The exception is where shellac was used to seal the surface.) Similarly, if the old cabinets were painted, be sure to use the same type of paint–latex or oil–as was originally used.

For staining cabinets, have I prepared the surface? ☐ yes   ☐ no

If you are going to restain the cabinets with a different color of finish, it will probably be necessary to remove the original finish. This can be done through a combination of sanding and chemical peel. Be aware, however, that the removal process is arduous, and if you're attempting it yourself, you may find halfway through that it's easier just to buy new! On the other hand, there are many stain products (such as Watco's Danish Finish) available that can go over almost any original stain and brighten it, in some cases making it look like new.

Will I paint or stain inside the cabinets?   ☐ **yes**   ☐ **no**

For most people, the assumption is that it's only necessary to renovate the exterior of the cabinets. After all, nobody looks inside. The problem, of course, is that people do look inside every time you open the cabinet doors. My suggestion is that if you're restaining or repainting your cabinets, you should plan on doing the inside as well. Of course, you don't need to do nearly as good a job. Typically, you can get away with a latex paint rolled on. But having newly painted cabinet interiors will only enhance the overall appearance.

Is there any repair work I need to do first?   ☐ **yes**   ☐ **no**

If you're planning on salvaging your old cabinets, be sure to make them solid enough to handle any new countertop you may be planning to use. This means that after the old countertop is removed, and before restaining or repainting, go through the cabinets and shore them up. A screw here and there can help enormously. You may need to add extra wood supports or metal braces. It is not uncommon to remove all the doors and reinstall with new hardware. Don't assume that just because they've been there for decades, old cabinets are solid. They may have originally been constructed poorly, or the demolition of the countertop may have weakened them. Plan on repairing as needed.

For laminating cabinets, do I have any preparation work?   ☐ **yes**   ☐ **no**

If you're having your existing cabinets laminated, there's probably the least interruption of your normal routines. Laminators often can do their work without having you even empty out your cabinets. They typically come in once for measurements, then show up several weeks later with new doors. They then spend a day or so laminating new wood onto the existing cabinets, attaching the new doors, and are done. Nevertheless, you may be asked to sand the cabinets, remove the contents from some, and clear counters and work areas.

Questions to Ask Your Contractor

Will you handle cabinet installation?   ☐ yes   ☐ no

If you're having a GC (general contractor) do your renovation, ask that person if he or she does cabinet installation. Don't assume that contractors do this. They may subcontract it out. If that's the case, you may find it less expensive to have the cabinet supplier or builder do the installation. Or you may want to handle the installation yourself. If the GC does the installation, it may be part of your overall renovation package and may or may not be listed as a separate item. It's something that should enter into your discussions regarding overall costs.

Are there particular brands you recommend?   ☐ yes   ☐ no

Renovation contractors who are experienced have the benefit of seeing not only hundreds of different jobs, but also of having installed hundreds of different types of cabinets. They may be able to steer you toward or away from cabinets that would present installation problems. They can warn you about cabinets that, once installed, do not hold up. It's unfortunate but true that sometimes the most ideal cabinet in our minds may turn out to be one that really isn't well built. Your contractor may be able to tune you into this.

Can you get me a deal on cabinets?   ☐ yes   ☐ no

Contractors who specialize in renovation work often establish close bonds with cabinet distributors and manufacturers. Many times they get a wholesale rate on the purchase. The question then becomes whether or not the contractor will pass the savings on to you. This can be done in two ways. Either the overall bid can be lower, reflecting the bargain the contractor is getting, or your cost of purchasing the cabinets can be reduced, reflecting the contractor's better price. One thing is certain, however. Unless you ask about the savings that could be possible, you aren't likely going to get them.

How long will it take to install?   ☐ yes   ☐ no

There's a big time difference between having a contractor install cabinets and doing it yourself. A contractor can typically get all the cabinets in a kitchen installed within a day or two. On the other hand, it could take you a week or longer. Be sure that you and your contractor are on the same track. If you're doing the installation, he or she will need to allot appropriate time for it. If the contractor is doing the work, you'll need to know how long it will take so you can schedule any other work or home duties around it.

Are there any problem "fixes" with the cabinets I've chosen?   ☐ yes   ☐ no

Your contractor may be familiar with the design and manufacturer of the cabinets you've selected. As noted earlier, he or she may be able to inform you of problems with installation, or later appearance, or how well they usually hold up. More importantly, the contractor may have "fixes" available that he or she can use to overcome these problems. Sometimes contractors can add extra wood bracing where they know a weakness is located. Or they can arrange cabinets in a different order to make doors less likely to bang into one another. Be sure to connect with your contractor about any comments he or she may have regarding the cabinets you've selected.

Are the cabinets I want appropriate for my countertop?   ☐ yes   ☐ no

It's important to understand that not all cabinets are suitable for all countertops. It mostly has to do with weight. While all countertops are heavy, some are far heavier than others. For example, most people consider laminate (Formica®) countertops to be fairly light because the laminate material itself is lightweight. However, it is glued onto pressed wood, which tends to be heavy. Even tile is very heavy, particularly if the base for it is a layer of cement. However, the heaviest countertops tend to be stone-granite. As a result, the cabinets you select must be able to withstand the weight of the countertops you choose. Manufacturers usually can tell you how much their cabinets can support. It's trickier renovating existing countertops. Here, your contractor may be able to show you how to build additional supports to withstand the weight of the countertop you choose. The biggest mistake, of course, is to select badly and have your cabinets sag, or worse, break. Think of all that money gone to waste!

8
Installing Countertops

Questions to Ask Yourself

Do I want new countertops in my kitchen or bath?   ☐ yes   ☐ no

The countertop is what most people look at. It's what tells whether you have a modern kitchen/bath, or an outdated one. If you're considering renovating a kitchen or bath, then I suggest that you give serious consideration to putting in a new countertop. Indeed, if you're putting in new cabinets, it's almost a necessity to put in a new countertop, as the old will normally be destroyed in the cabinet installation process. This is not an area to skimp on.

Can I repair my existing countertops?   ☐ yes   ☐ no

Only consider this if you're not putting in new cabinets. If your current counter is stone (granite), it may indeed be well worth saving. Contact a refinisher about resanding and sealing the surface if it's stained. I've never seen old laminate with burns or other blemishes successfully refinished. Older Corian® by DuPont can frequently have burns or other marks cut out and reblended. However, consider that the color may be outdated. For old tile, if you like the tile itself (color and style) consider having it regrouted. Here, a layer of the old grout is removed and new grout put in its place. The problem is that removing the old grout can cause old tile to chip.

Have I checked new countertops on the Internet and in magazines?   ☐ yes   ☐ no

Before you begin, check to see what's available to you. Today, countertop manufacturers advertise widely in magazines and almost all have their own websites where you can see their products. They can also direct you to local dealers who have showrooms where the products are on display. Don't make a hasty decision based on information you gathered the last time you considered doing such a project. Times and materials have changed dramatically. There may be something new out there today that you had never dreamed existed and that will perfectly fulfill your need. But if you don't go looking for it, you won't find it.

Have I checked out new countertops at building supply stores?   ☐ yes   ☐ no

Quite frankly, there's a lot of profit in putting in counter-tops, and as a result, most building supply stores have model kitchens displaying the wares of a variety of man-ufacturers and products. Be sure to check these out. There are also showrooms dedicated to kitchen and bath where you can get ideas. Check your local yellow pages. Just remember, however, that the showroom prices may not be the lowest you can get, even on the same or similar products. Ask your contractor if he or she can get dis-counts. Be sure to check with other suppliers and on the Internet for discounts.

Have I gone to tile stores?   ☐ yes   ☐ no

Some tile manufacturers (Dal, for example) maintain their own stores. In them they display a wide range of prod-ucts, some in model kitchen and bath settings. It can be well worth your time to check these out for ideas. But as noted previously, keep in mind that your contractor may be able to get better prices. Also, be sure that whatever tile you choose, it's readily available. Tile comes from around the world–Italy, Mexico, even China. If you select a tile that won't be available for six months, you could put your renovation project on serious hold.

Have I gone to quarries?

☐ yes ☐ no

Stone is sold by the individual piece. And no two pieces are exactly alike. When you're in a building supply store, you may see small samples of stone. But keep in mind that these are just to give you an idea of the color and texture that stone comes in. The actual pieces that these samples were taken from are long gone. The only way you can get a piece of stone and know for sure what it's going to be like is to go to the quarry and pick it out. There, the stone is set up in rows for you to examine. You pick the one you like, and that same piece is the one that will be installed. Be sure you pick a piece that's large enough for your needs. Note that the term "quarry" here is a misnomer. In most cases, what we're talking about is a store that sells stone that was, in fact, quarried hundreds if not thousands of miles away. This is not to say that true quarries don't sell their own stone—they do. But typically they have a very small selection, limited to what they can get out of the ground right there.

Have I comparison shopped tile, laminate, plastic, and stone?

☐ yes ☐ no

If you want to get the top product, chances are it will cost you a lot for tile, plastic, or stone. Laminate is usually cheaper regardless of grade. However, if you're looking to get a much lower price, then you're probably better off shopping for tile. Tile offers the broadest price range, from under $1 a tile to as much as $50 a tile and more. Stone is generally sold by the inch. And plastic is sold based on the total square footage of the kitchen counter. It can be helpful to create a comparison chart *after* you've picked your choices in each. As I said, don't be surprised if the final prices for all the materials are similar.

How big a backsplash will I want?

☐ yes ☐ no

A backsplash is just what it says it is—it's made up of the countertop material, only set vertically behind it to catch any water (or food or other kitchen materials) that accidentally splashes up. The cost of the backsplash is just as much as for the countertop. Therefore, you can increase or decrease your building materials costs by increasing or decreasing the size of your backsplash. Keep in mind that while an 18-inch backsplash is really nice, with granite sold by the inch, it could cost you thousands more than a 6-inch backsplash, which might be adequate.

Questions to Ask Yourself If You're Doing the Tile

Have I comparison shopped for color and style?   ☐ yes   ☐ no

If you haven't shopped for tile in the last five years, get ready for a treat. It has undergone a revolution. In addition to the American, Italian, and Mexican tiles that long have been available, there are now stone, cement, synthetic, even high-tech plastic and glass tiles. Of course, their prices tend to be high, but the quality and selection in color and design is amazing. If you're doing it yourself, however, a big consideration is the difficulty in installation. Be sure to check with the manufacturer as to what special techniques must be used. While most tile is set with "quick-set," some requires special mastic or exotic glues. Sometimes you may want to base your selection more on ease of installation than on color and style!

Have I studied how to install tile?   ☐ yes   ☐ no

Anyone can install tile. But not everyone can do it well. However, the techniques required for installation can be learned. There are many books on the market that show you step by step how to lay tile properly. (You may want to check out my book, *Tips and Traps When Renovating Your Home* for the basic steps.) Just keep in mind that you want to keep your lines straight, your counter top flat, and your tile spaced evenly. One last tip is to get a good cutter. While experts can quickly lay tile using a device that first scores and breaks pieces, most beginners find a diamond-bladed saw the easiest way to make accurate cuts. And these can be inexpensively rented.

Have I taken accurate measurements?   ☐ yes   ☐ no

Once again, measure twice, cut once. The only way to know how much tile you'll need is to get accurate area measurements. You'll also need to measure how much bull-nose or other edge tiles you'll need, how many corner pieces, and so on. And when you're marking a piece to be cut, be sure to lay it in place to see that the cut mark is exactly where you want it to be. Once cut, you can't put tile back together again. Most stores will let you return uncut pieces, so the best advice is to buy more of everything. That way you won't run out in the middle of the job. And you'll return the excess later.

Have I purchased the necessary tools?   ☐ yes   ☐ no

Tile work requires a variety of specialized tools. These include nippers (for breaking off small pieces), a diamond-blade wet saw, notched trowel (for spreading adhesive), rubber-faced trowel (for grouting), and a host of other common tools including a utility knife, tape measure, straight edge, sponge, safety glasses, rubber gloves and mallet, rags, chalk line, buckets, level, and framing square. Yes, you will probably need *all* of the above, and more. The good news is that with the exception of the diamond-blade wet saw, all of the items are relatively inexpensive. Most, including the saw, can be rented from building supply stores and building materials rental outlets.

Do I have enough tile, adhesive, and grout?   ☐ yes   ☐ no

As noted, buy more rather than less. Most people buy too little tile and too much adhesive and grout. When it comes to adhesive, the most common bonding agent is "thinset," which you can buy in dry 25- and 50-pound sacks for a nominal amount. The price quickly goes up if you buy premixed thinset in a can, and when you get to special epoxy mastics, it can cost $20 a can or more. For most applications, however, the basic dry thinset will do. Check the product label if you're going to have underwater (as in a shower), wet (as near a sink), or vertical applications. Most grout is likewise inexpensive when purchased in bulk. Sometimes you can get a slight price reduction in tile purchased in large quantities. However, you best bet is to get a builder's discount.

Have I laid down a starting line?   ☐ yes   ☐ no

The single most common mistake that beginners make when laying tile is to start at a corner or side edge instead of the middle or front. Starting near the center or front results in edges and ends that are evenly balanced. It also helps ensure that the tile goes down straight. A starting line typically is a straight chalk line drawn across the widest portion of the counter. A line perpendicular to it forms the axis were the first tile will go. Be sure that the chalk lines are parallel to the edges of the counter. You may also want to use pencil instead of chalk at some point, as the chalk quickly disappears.

Do I have a good cutting device?   ☐ yes   ☐ no

As noted, a diamond-blade wet saw is easiest to use for beginners. However, a snapper, which scribes a line and then breaks the tile along it, works as well in most cases, though it is harder for a beginner to use. Nippers cut off small pieces of tile. A small file for smoothing a rough edge can also be helpful. The key, of course, is to make as few cuts as possible. The fewer cuts, the less time spent and the less chance of breaking tile.

Have I prepared my base?   ☐ yes   ☐ no

Ideally, your base will begin with plywood. On top of that you can spread an impervious membrane so water won't get through to damage cabinets beneath. Above that is typically wire mesh, and over that a bed of mortar is used to flatten and even out the surface perfectly. Adhesive goes on the mortar, and tile is affixed to the adhesive. For quicker and easier work, a prepared cement slab such as Wonder Board can be used in place of the mortar bed. However, you won't be able to make it as level as if you used mortar.

Do I know how to use adhesive? ☐ **yes** ☐ **no**

The can or sack of adhesive will tell you how to mix (if necessary) and apply it. Follow directions to the letter. If they indicate that after initial mixing you need to let the adhesive "rest" for a time, follow the guidelines closely. This is an important step in helping it to set up. Be sure to use a notched trowel with the notch sizes recommended for the adhesive. Don't simply feel that any notched trowel will do–it won't. Be sure to cover all of the bed with the adhesive. Any areas that you don't cover are areas where the tile won't adhere. Be sure to be careful where you let the adhesive spatter. It can be a nuisance to clean up. Don't get it on top of the tile. After it hardens, it can be almost impossible to remove.

Do I know how to maintain straight lines? ☐ **yes** ☐ **no**

Your initial line should be drawn on your base. After that, maintain equal distances between tiles using plastic separators (readily available at tile stores). The easiest way to check lines is to get your eye down to the end of a line and sight along it. You should be able to tell quickly if the line bends or if any of the tiles are too close or too far apart. Sighting along lines is probably the best way to keep your lines straight, although you can certainly use other means such as a straight edge or square.

Have I chosen the correct grout? ☐ **yes** ☐ **no**

Grout has both texture and color. You want to be sure that both are correct. If you chose a prepared grout (selected from samples), you can be fairly sure that the grout will turn out the same color as you want. If, however, you prepare the grout yourself, then the only way to be sure that it will turn out the right color is to let some dry and see how it looks. One person I know mixed grout for his kitchen countertop and half way through ran out. So he mixed a second batch. When dry, however, the second batch was distinctly a different color from the first! Grout also will have texture depending on how much sand is added. Grout without sand is commonly used for tiles set very close together. Tile with sand, giving it a gritty look and feel, is used for tiles set wide apart. The sand helps the grout stick together better. Be sure to let the grout "slake" or rest the prescribed time before using it. This will help it to set up properly later on.

Have I quickly removed excess grout? ☐ **yes** ☐ **no**

Keep in mind that grout is intended to stick to tile. If you get it on top of the tile, it may stick just as well as if you get it on the bottom. So be sure to clean off any excess grout as soon as possible. Initially, you will do this with a rubber trowel, which you'll use to squeeze the grout into its grooves. It will take off all of the large pieces and leave a film on the tile. Let the film dry for half an hour or so and remove it with a clean cloth. The tiles themselves may be cleaned further after the grout dries. The biggest mistake that beginners usually make when applying grout is to leave too much in the grooves. You don't want it bubbling up over the edge of the tile. Ideally, you want it to end up being just below the lip of the tile. If you leave too much grout in the groove and let it dry, it's there for the duration of the countertop.

Questions to Ask Yourself If You're Doing the Laminate

Have I double-checked my measurements? ☐ **yes** ☐ **no**

Assuming that you're having the plastic material laminated to the pressed wood countertop surface, your biggest job is getting accurate measurements. (Some people will glue the laminate to the wood themselves. There's nothing wrong with doing this. Keep in mind, however, that it requires that you get the glue to adhere evenly, that you get out all bubbles, and that you get a clean cut on the edges.) The company that's selling you the finished laminated countertop will often come in and take its own measurements because they are so crucial. If, however, you are to take your own, be sure that you follow their guidelines precisely. And measure accurately down to a sixteenth of an inch or closer. With premade laminate countertops, being off by even a hair can mean that they won't line up right in the kitchen, the seams will unduly show, or they won't fit properly on top of the cabinets.

Will I have the laminated countertop delivered? ☐ yes ☐ no

Assuming that you're not doing the laminating yourself (which is something I don't recommend you do unless you're experienced at it), you'll need to get the countertops from the shop to your home. Try to have the shop deliver them. They are used to handling long, heavy tops and undoubtedly have a truck set up just for this purpose. If you try to get them yourself, even if you have a pickup truck, chances are something will get bumped, dented, or scratched. Remember, it's the final appearance that's crucial, and if you have to pay an extra 50 bucks to get the top delivered in good shape, it's well worth it.

Do I have someone to help me put the counter in place? ☐ yes ☐ no

This is definitely a two-person job. I have seen guys who thought they were big and tough try to maneuver the laminate tops into place by themselves. It's not a pretty sight. And it doesn't necessarily get easier once the counter is on top of the cabinets. The top still needs to be wiggled around—one person holding while the other person clamps or drills. Be sure you ask a strong friend to assist you at this crucial juncture. If you assemble the countertop pieces incorrectly, the lines will show badly, not to mention other areas that may be off.

Have I braced my cabinets? ☐ yes ☐ no

Frequently, laminate is the best choice to go over existing cabinets. But regardless of whether the cabinets are brand new or old, you should check to be sure they are sturdy. While the weight from the countertop is directed straight down, you should also brace against lateral movement, in case someone leans heavily against the cabinets or top. Keep in mind when bracing that the type of wood you use isn't really important (as long as it's strong) because it won't show. Also be sure to leave clearance for opening doors and gaining access to shelves.

Questions to Ask the Contractor About Choosing Tile

Will you install the tile I've selected?   ☐ yes   ☐ no

Don't assume that the contractor will automatically install whatever tile you choose. Some pieces have harder installations than others. Some tiles have a tendency to chip or break easily. And for these reasons and others, some contractors may balk. Be sure that you and your contractor are in agreement on the tile. If not, you may have to select a different tile . . . or a different contractor!

Will you buy the tile for me?   ☐ yes   ☐ no

You can go to the store and select just the tile you want. But when it comes time to purchase the tile, you should ask the contractor if he or she will make the purchase. The reason is the contractor's discount. Typically, contractors will get 10 to 40 percent off the retail price, depending on where and what they buy. If you are dealing directly with the tile person, this discount should be passed on to you. If, however, you are working with a general contractor who has subcontracted the tile work, don't necessarily expect to have the savings passed on to you. The savings will probably go to the GC who may or may not have passed them along in the overall job price.

How widely do you suggest spacing the tiles?   ☐ yes   ☐ no

Tiles can be spaced directly next to each other, or as much as half an inch apart. The amount of spacing helps determine the overall look of the finished tile work. My suggestion is that you ask an expert what type of spacing would look best for the tile you've selected. That expert could be the person who sold you the tile. But it's even better to ask the person who is laying the tile. The tile contractor will have had experience with different types of tile and different widths, and will be able to suggest what might look best in your case. Keep in mind that both very narrow and very wide spacing ends up with grout that is hard to keep clean.

What color grout do you suggest?

☐ yes ☐ no

You may have your heart set on white grout. But your tile person could suggest that with the color of tile you've selected, gray or brown might look better. Consider it carefully. Additionally, keep in mind that no matter what color grout you get, over time it will get dirty and discolored. White looks terrific at first, but when it discolors, it turns gray. What's worse is that it never discolors evenly. Rather, heavily used parts turn first leaving your tile countertop with a partially white and partially gray grout. Colored grouts also get dirty, but with the exception of black, they tend to show it less.

Will you seal the grout?

☐ yes ☐ no

Your best defense against having your grout absorb food, dirt, water, and whatever else happens to be on your counter (and thus, discoloring) is sealer. Grout is naturally porous. Sealer, typically a silicone mixture, gets down into the grout and helps produce a repellent surface. Putting the sealer on is not difficult, but the tile contractor is the best person to do it. Remember, since the sealer normally can't be put on until a couple of days after the grout is applied, it requires an extra trip back, and many tile contractors simply don't want to spend the extra time and effort. Try to get your tile contractor to do it.

What sealer will you use?

☐ yes ☐ no

I've had tile contractors tell me that it really doesn't matter what type or brand of sealer you use. They say that all brands use silicone and they all work about the same. However, having done this a great many times, I can assure you that this is baloney. Yes, most sealers are about the same, and they all do a rather poor job. They require many coats, and even after all of that, the grout still quickly stains. However, while I make no guarantees, I have found one product that I am particularly happy with. For me, it works three times better than any other sealer I've used. Unfortunately, it's also three times more expensive. (Expect to pay between $30 and $50 for a small quart of it!) It's called Sealer's Choice by Aqua Mix of

Sante Fe Springs, California. Don't expect to find it at your local building supply store, however, since it's usually sold only commercially. Your tile contractor should be able to get it for you.

___

Will you handle bull-nosed edges?   ☐ yes   ☐ no

There are all sorts of edges that can be used with tile. Some are relatively easy to install. Others are more difficult. Some require two or three pieces of tile to make up the edge. Be sure that you discuss the type of edging you want with your tile contractor and that he or she is willing and able to install it for you. There may even be an extra installation charge for fancier edges.

___

What about inserting accent pieces?   ☐ yes   ☐ no

It has become fashionable to install accent tile pieces here and there on a countertop. These can be in the form of flowers, birds, butterflies, or almost anything else. Indeed, in many areas there's a kind of cottage industry of people who bake any image you want onto whatever tiles you've purchased. The accent piece can add charm and distinctiveness to otherwise dull tile. However, it's important that you and your tile contractor agree on where they are to go. My suggestion is that you listen to your tile contractor tell you where he or she wants to place them, and then you make the final decision yourself. This is particularly the case when you have a mural or other multitile piece of accent art to install into a countertop.

___

Will you install the sink and stove?   ☐ yes   ☐ no

The sink should be installed by the tile contractor. The stove rarely is, although depending on the type of stove and installation procedure, you may want a contractor to do it as well. Sinks usually come in two styles: flush mount and surface mount. In a flush mount sink, the tile butts right up to the edge of the sink so that you can simply wash scraps and water into the sink. In a surface or "over the top" mount, the sink actually sits right on top of the tile. In theory, the surface mount can be put in any time after the tile is finished, but if the tile contractor puts it in place, he or she can grout around it for a nice, matching fit. Be aware that installing the sink does not include installing the fixtures (faucet, disposal, drain, and so on), which is something you or a plumber will need to do.

When will you do the job?

☐ **yes** ☐ **no**

If you have a GC, he or she will take care of timing. However, if you're dealing directly with the tile or masonry contractor, then you'll have to make your own arrangements. Be aware that good tile contractors are always busy. Frequently, the earliest they can fit you in will be within a month after you ask them for a date. Thus, plan on asking them a month before you need them. Check with the tile contractor you've chosen to see what his or her schedule is like, and plan accordingly.

How long will it take?

☐ **yes** ☐ **no**

Tiling goes quickly. Unless you have an exceptionally large kitchen, it can typically be done in a couple of days. If you are told that it's going to take a week or several weeks, then beware. Your tile contractor may be trying to fit you into several jobs that he or she is doing simultaneously. That often means that none of the jobs get the detailed attention it deserves, and you might be better off looking for another tile contractor. In a small to medium-sized kitchen, for example, there's typically one day to remove the existing countertop (if that hasn't already been done) and to prepare the new counter, and a second day to finish the counter and to lay the tile and grout. And if necessary, a third day may be needed to finish up. Of course, the bigger the job, the longer it can take.

Will you handle all demolition and clean-up?

☐ **yes** ☐ **no**

Tile contractors are used to not only laying tile, but also to removing existing countertops. Therefore, they are the perfect people to handle this demolition. Indeed, you may want to wait on having the old countertop removed until your tile person comes in. Be aware, however, that demolition is a dirty, dangerous, and difficult job. This is particularly the case when the old countertop is tile that must be broken up with a sledgehammer. It produces sharp pieces that can easily cause wounds. And the tile, cement base, and other parts of the countertop are extremely heavy. In short, this is a job that it would be wise for you to pay an expert to handle.

How long will it be before I can use the tile? ☐ yes ☐ no

This will depend on the type of grout, adhesive, and sealer used. Your tile contractor will be able to tell you how long it will be before the tile can be washed, and that indicates when you can use it. If it's up to you to seal the grout, then I would strictly follow the instructions on the sealer. It will tell you how many coats to apply and how long to wait after application before using the countertop. Typically, you can use the countertop almost immediately. However, until it's sealed, the grout is easily stained.

Will you come back and fix any cracks? ☐ yes ☐ no

With tile, don't expect a perfect job, even if you have the best contractor in the world. Over time, homes settle, cabinets shift, and cracks appear in the grout, and possibly even in tiles. This should rarely be the case in the countertop itself, since if properly prepared, the counter will have a solid plywood base over which wire mesh and a coat of mortar have been laid. More likely it will appear in the corners between the countertop and the splashboard and in areas where there is physical stress, like at the edges of sinks. A good tile contractor will agree to come back within six months and fix any broken tile or cracks that occur, usually without charge to you.

Questions to Ask the Contractor About Putting In Laminate

Will you buy the countertops based on your measurements? ☐ yes ☐ no

As noted earlier, measurements for laminate countertops are crucial. If measured correctly, allowing for backsplash and other features of the top, it should fit perfectly. Any slight deviations in measurement, however, could mean that the premade top will not properly fit. Be sure that your contractor agrees to do his or her own measurements and to stick by them, even if that means having to reorder the top.

Will you guarantee minimal grooves?   ☐ yes   ☐ no

The bane of laminate countertops is the grooves that show. Since the laminate comes in large pieces, it is necessary to create grooves where these pieces join. Typically they are diagonals at corners. However, they could also be right in the middle of a counter, if inadequate planning was done. Be sure that your contractor specifies where the grooves will be, that they will be at corners or other logical locations, and that they are held to a minimum.

Will you install the sink and stove?   ☐ yes   ☐ no

For laminate countertops, the sink may use a metal ring for a nearly flush installation, or may simply lay on top of the counter in a lip installation. To fit, the hole for the sink must be cut precisely. Be sure your contractor does this for you. The same can hold true for the stove, although today many stoves are freestanding or slide-ins. The whole idea here is to have a finish that looks professionally done, and who better to do this than your contractor?

Questions to Ask Your Contractor About Putting In Stone

Do you have a particular quarry you recommend?   ☐ yes   ☐ no

Stone, such as granite or marble, requires a specialist for installation. These are people who are used to handling the great weight of the countertop and who know how to place it properly. Note that even though granite is extremely strong, if it's improperly installed, it can crack. Once cracked, there is no repairing it—the broken piece must be removed and a new piece installed. Your contractor, therefore, should be a pro, and as such will likely know the best quarries in your area. Ask for his or her advice here. He or she may even steer you toward certain slabs that will look better and/or have better prices.

Will you guarantee the installation?   ☐ yes   ☐ no

If you break a piece of tile, it's nothing to replace it. If you burn a Corian countertop, you can meld the section and remove the burn. But if you drop a piece of granite and it cracks, you can throw it away. And as noted above, if you install it incorrectly and it cracks, it's worthless. Therefore, it's a good idea to get a written guarantee on the installation from the contractor. This guarantee should be for a long time, many years. After all, granite itself is hundreds of thousands of years old. What are a few more years in your kitchen? If the contractor is unwilling to give a guarantee, you should find one who is.

Will you seal the stone?   ☐ yes   ☐ no

Contrary to popular opinion, granite is not impervious. Rather, it's a fairly porous stone. That means that if you pour chocolate syrup or tomato paste or wine on the surface, the liquid can penetrate at least the upper layers of the granite and become imbedded there. If that happens, there's no washing the stain out. Depending on how deep it went, in fact, there may be no getting it out. Therefore, granite should be sealed. While this is not a highly technical job, it's something that the contractor should do for you, at least the first time. After that, you may want to seal it yourself every year or so. Note that even though the granite comes with a highly polished finish, sealing is still usually a good idea.

Questions to Ask Your Contractor About Putting In Corian

Are you certified?   ☐ **yes**   ☐ **no**

Corian is a popular synthetic countertop manufactured by DuPont. It comes in sheets and is extremely durable. The sheets can be "melded" together so that the final countertop has no seams at all. In years past, the color and style of Corian was quite limited, but today these have been enormously expanded. However, installation of Corian requires an expert, someone who has been specially trained and certified by DuPont. Be sure that your contractor has the background to install Corian properly for you. When done well, it produces a marvelous look. And when blended with other materials, such as tile and even granite, it can look elegant.

Do you guarantee the installation?   ☐ **yes**   ☐ **no**

It should go without saying that the installer should guarantee the installation. However, if it looks great when it's finished, chances are it will continue to look that way. Keep in mind, however, that Corian can be damaged. It can get burns and other nicks and discolorations. The good news, however, is that these can be cut out, a new piece installed over the damaged area, and that blended into the whole. To facilitate this, a good installer will leave an extra slab of the original behind so that you will have a perfect match for fixing any damages. Typically, this is attached at the bottom or back of the sink. Be sure your installer does this and tells you where the extra piece is. Also ask if he or she offers a discount over the next five years for fixing any damaged areas that you cause. Some do, and keeping this in mind can save you a lot of money later on. Also, DuPont offers a limited 10-year warranty on the product, and in some cases, on the installation. Check out *http://www.corianwhysettle.com*.

9
Putting In New Floors

Questions to Ask Yourself

Do I want wood floors?

yes   no

For many people, wood is the ultimate material to use on a floor. It fairly shouts beauty and richness. Therefore, when renovating, it's often a first choice. Keep in mind, however, that wood flooring today is among the most expensive you can get. This is particularly the case if you opt for oak or some of the more exotic hardwoods. Also, although it looks wonderful in kitchen and bath areas, if you get a plumbing leak and water gets underneath, it can quickly buckle, warp, and a very expensive floor can be quickly destroyed. So from a practical standpoint, wood flooring in potentially wet areas doesn't make sense. From an aesthetic perspective, however, many people simply do it anyway!

Will I be happy with a composite floor?

yes   no

There are many of these available, Pergo® probably being the most well known. These are usually composed of a hardened material onto which a woodlike surface is laminated. This is bonded to a pressed wood base. The floor is then "floated" above the existing floor with each board glued to its neighbor and all held in place at the edges. These floors are about half the price of real wood, and to save even more money, many people feel that they can install their own composite flooring. Some successfully do just that. However, it is tricky and I suggest you take a class on installation (sometimes available from the manufacturer—check websites for times and locations) before attempting it.

Do I want tile on my floors?

☐ **yes**   ☐ **no**

Tile comes in so many different varieties these days, that it has regained its role as one of the leading flooring materials. While the smaller 4- and 6-inch tiles are frequently used on countertops; the large 12- and 16-inch tile squares are frequently used on floors. While the choice of color, texture, and design is almost endless, it's important to note that some of these come with a surface that is designed to be nonskid, even when wet. If you are able to put tile on your cabinets, you should be able to do the same thing with your floors. The only difference is that you'll get sore knees and ankles from all the bending! The application process is essentially the same.

Will I be happy with linoleum?

☐ **yes**   ☐ **no**

Today's linoleums are strikingly different from those of only a few years ago. They are offered in both a type of cushioned (soft) floor and in a very hard surface, as well as in a rainbow of colors, designs, and patterns. Good linoleum floors can last a long time (10 years or more) and they can be a fraction of the cost of wood, stone, or tile, so many budget-conscious renovators opt for them. Keep in mind, however, that linoleum in sheets does require expert installation. Unless you have a large, relatively square room with no difficult corners, you shouldn't try it yourself. Beware of linoleum (vinyl) squares that offer the appearance of easy installation. (After all, you just lay one square at a time, and they even come with adhesive backing!) While installation may seem easy, there are many potential problems (like adhesive getting on the top surface, crooked lines, and nonadhering tiles, to name a few) including the fact that over time, dirt and grime tends to settle in the many groves between the linoleum tiles giving them a dirty appearance.

Do I want to put granite or marble on my floors?

☐ **yes**   ☐ **no**

These are by far the most expensive and elegant of floors. While marble is generally considered too porous a material for a countertop, it is sometimes used on floors. Granite is rarely used in this fashion although I have seen some spectacular entranceways and staircases created from granite, and in one case, from Corian! If you can afford stone floors, you can afford expert installation. Don't attempt it yourself. Also pay attention to the finish. Stone can be highly polished, but that also makes it very slippery. Usually a rougher finish is more practical.

Will I want wall-to-wall carpeting?   ☐ yes   ☐ no

Make this decision early on. For many renovators, wall-to-wall carpeting is the standard by which all other floors are measured. If you're one of these, then don't bother putting wood, tile, marble, or any other finished flooring down. Just put down a plywood subfloor or cement slab. Since no one will see it, what goes under the carpeting doesn't matter. Nylon is still the most popular carpeting, although the various other synthetics and natural fibers have their attractions. Check with a good carpet store for the plusses and minuses of each. And be careful of the color. For a quick sale, real estate agents recommend white or a very light color. However, if you're the one living in the house, you'll find yourself constantly taking off your shoes trying to avoid getting the carpeting dirty. And it will soil despite your best efforts. For impressive looks, go with plush and a light color. For practicality, go with a multilevel, more colorful carpet.

Can my old wood floors be sanded and restained?   ☐ yes   ☐ no

If you have wood floors in your house, try to save them. If they can be resurrected, you'll save yourself thousands of dollars . . . and you may end up with a beautiful floor to boot. In much older homes, softwoods such as pines were frequently used. In homes from the middle of the last century, oak usually was the wood of choice. Often the planking is wide or of irregular sizes, which offers a beautiful look. Regardless of the wood used, ask a professional if it can be sanded. This involves using a huge sanding machine to take off about a 16th of an inch off the surface. The original stain goes with the top. A big problem could happen if the floorboards were top-nailed (good installation has them side-nailed), thus preventing sanding unless the nails are first removed or countersunk. This often leaves dark marks in the flooring, which may or may not be attractive. Once sanded, original floors can be stained to a variety of colors.

Can my old tile floors be saved?

☐ **yes**   ☐ **no**

If you have existing tile floors, before deciding to replace them, see if they can be saved. Many installers will also do repairs, including regrouting. The biggest problem comes from cracked and broken tiles. While these can easily be removed, the hard part is finding new tiles to match. Sometimes, if all of the broken tiles are at the edges of the floor, a pattern of new tiles can be worked around the old. This is a situation where being creative can save thousands of dollars and can come up with some unusual and attractive patterns and colors.

Do I have asbestos tile floors?

☐ **yes**   ☐ **no**

Many old floors contain asbestos. This is usually the case when the tiles are vinyl squares and the flooring was put in decades ago. A good tile installer can usually tell if your floor has asbestos tile. If it does, you will need to use a special asbestos abatement company to have it removed, and the cost will be very high. However, encapsulation is usually acceptable for treating asbestos. That means that if you can "bury" the asbestos floor under a new, permanent floor, you may be able to avoid removing it. For example, installing a new synthetic floor such as Pergo might solve the problem.

Have I checked out new floors in magazines and online?

☐ **yes**   ☐ **no**

Don't reinvent the wheel. See what others have done in terms of flooring. House and home magazines are excellent sources of information here. Their pictures always show floors. What creative things have others done? In addition to getting ideas, you often will be given the websites of the various manufacturers, and these can lead to other creative flooring ideas, not to mention the local addresses of retailers.

Have I checked out new floors at building supply stores?   ☐ yes   ☐ no

Unfortunately, building supply stores do not usually do as good a job with displaying flooring as they do with counters and cabinets. And they may not carry as wide a selection as you would like. Keep in mind that there are hundreds of flooring manufacturers, not just the two or three that any given building supply store may carry. And prices and selection are all over the chart. Again, check the Internet using keyword "flooring" for dealers.

Have I created a price comparison list?   ☐ yes   ☐ no

Unlike with countertops, where pricing across the board may be similar, with flooring, pricing offers a broad range, depending on what material and quality you select. It's important, however, to compare apples with apples, not oranges. When you've selected your four or five best options, write out not only their square-foot price (including installation), but also their advantages and negatives. For example, you may find oak boards are roughly twice the cost of synthetic flooring. On the other hand, to get the rich authentic look they offer and the solid feel under your feet, you may be willing to pay the extra cost.

Is the floor I want available?   ☐ yes   ☐ no

Availability is always the big bugaboo with regard to materials. You may find the perfect flooring at a great price, only to learn that the mill isn't shipping any more of it for nine months. Will you be willing to wait that long? Or is it now time to consider a reasonable alternative? When making your decision, don't forget to ask how soon you can get the flooring delivered to your home.

Questions to Ask Your Contractor

Will you handle floor installation?   ☐ yes   ☐ no

This usually depends on the type of flooring you are using. General contractors often will handle wood flooring themselves, but will hire out tile, linoleum, and other floors. That's because they often come from a background of being carpenters and are used to working with wood, but not other materials. If your general contractor is doing the work himself or herself, you may be able to negotiate a good price for installation. However, if the general contractor is hiring a sub to do it, you'll have to pay both the sub's markup and the contractor's markup as well. You might be better off finding the sub and negotiating the work yourself.

Can you recommend an installer?   ☐ yes   ☐ no

An old rule in renovation is that good people know good people. If you once find a contractor (a GC or any sub) who does good work, he or she probably knows others who likewise do good work. If you're going to sub out the flooring yourself, be sure to ask for people whose work they like and respect for recommendations. One person leads to another, and very quickly you can put together a stable of contractors for not only flooring, but all the other aspects of the renovation that you will sub out yourself.

Are there particular floors that you recommend?   ☐ yes   ☐ no

While contractors all do a little bit of everything, most are really specialists. Even when it comes to one type of flooring, such as tile or wood, they may only be familiar with a small range of products from a small group of manufacturers. This can work to your advantage, *if* you ask them in advance what products they recommend, and *if* one or more of those products suits your needs. On the other hand, if your contractor doesn't work with the product you have your heart set on, you're better off finding a new contractor. In this case, check with the manufacturer for recommended installers.

Can you get me a deal on the flooring?   ☐ yes   ☐ no

Chances are you'll buy flooring once or twice in a lifetime. On the other hand, your contractor probably buys it regularly every month. Now, who is the manufacturer likely to cut a better deal to? Don't overlook the very real possibility that your contractor can save you money by buying the supplies, even though the retailer swears that no discounts are offered. You may be able to save 5 to 40 percent just by asking.

How long will it take to install?   ☐ **yes**   ☐ **no**

If you install the floor yourself, it can take days, sometimes agonizing weeks. I know; I've done it! On the other hand, a professional installer can have it done in an amazingly short time. After all, time is money to a contractor. The quicker a contractor completes your job, the sooner he or she can be off earning money at the next job. Nevertheless, no matter how quickly it can be done, it will still take time. And while the floors are being done, no one else can work on the project. (It's very difficult to get around a renovation site when you can't walk on the floors!) Find out not only how long it will take, but when the installer will start, and plan your other aspects of the renovation around this.

Are there any problems with the flooring that I've chosen?   ☐ **yes**   ☐ **no**

You might tell an installer, "I'm having 'X' tile installed throughout my kitchen, bath, and entranceway, and I'd like you to give me a price for putting it in." Okay, the contractor gives you a price. You like it, you do it, and you run into unforeseen problems. On the other hand, you could say, "I'm thinking of using 'X' tile. Have you used it before? Were there any problems with installation? Any problems afterward?" And the installer might say, "It's a terrible product. It scratches easily. You'll be very unhappy with it." It's far better to ask than to dictate to someone who's more expert than you.

10
Adding New Kitchen Appliances

Questions to Ask Yourself

Do my existing kitchen appliances work well?

☐ yes   ☐ no

The old adage, "If it ain't broke, don't fix it!" might apply here. Why spend money, time, and effort obtaining new appliances if the ones you have work perfectly? It's certainly something to consider, but also check the questions in this chapter on age, color, and style. On the other hand, very frequently kitchen appliances don't work as well as we'd like. An old gas range may have sticky valves. An oven may not keep the right temperature. A refrigerator may be energy inefficient. A dishwasher may be too loud. If your existing appliances don't work well, then now is the time to change them. Be sure to include the cost of replacing them in your overall renovation budget.

Are any of my appliances older than 10 years?

☐ yes   ☐ no

I recently had an old car (the make to remain anonymous) that had 105,000 miles on it. It worked like a charm, and when I had an opportunity to trade it in on a new one, my response was, "Why should I dump it when it runs so well?" The answer came before the car reached 106,000 when the engine blew. Appliances are a lot like cars. They tend to run well, until they drop dead. While no one can give the exact lifespan of any appliance, it's fairly safe to say that most last around 10 years or more. It's the "or more" where the uncertainty lies. If your appliances are already 10 years old, they are somewhat out-of-date. And as long as you're redoing your kitchen, now would be a great time simply to trade them out. Why wait until six months after your beautiful kitchen is done to have to go through again replacing appliances? Act while the iron is hot.

Are any of them the wrong color or style for my new kitchen?

☐ yes   ☐ no

Perhaps you have white appliances in your current kitchen that go great with your existing white cabinets. But you're getting new stained wood cabinets, and colored appliances would look oh so much better. Or perhaps your appliances are ultramodern in appearance, and you're putting in early American cabinets. A more conservative look in appliances would be better. Pay attention to the color and style of your new kitchen cabinets (and, of course, countertops and flooring). If they are dramatically different from the old (and I certainly hope they are, or else why go through the trouble and cost?!), then you should think about replacing appliances as well.

Do I have gas/electric/drain/water hookups where they're needed?

☐ yes   ☐ no

People who have gas ranges inevitably want electric. And those who have electric want gas. And in the new kitchen, the sink will go on the opposite side of where it is now . . . or perhaps in a new island in the center. As soon as we start renovating a kitchen, we begin placing appliances where we want to them to go, not necessarily where they are now. The trouble is that appliances need hookups from 220 volts for electric ovens and ranges, to natural gas outlets, to sanitary drains and water supplies. The question now becomes, can you easily and inexpensively put in new hookups where you want the new appliances to go? It's a truism that you can put hookups anywhere, if you're willing to pay the price. But if it involves digging up a foundation or slab, you may find that the $10,000 to $15,000 extra it costs to put your new stove eight feet over from where the old one is, just isn't worth it. Check to see how much new hookups will cost you before you lay your plans in concrete.

Do I need a special permit?   ☐ **yes**   ☐ **no**

If you are simply unplugging one oven and installing another, then you probably don't need a building permit. The exception here is for dishwashers and water heaters where most cities require a permit for every change, since it could effect the drinking water quality (or the gas/electric hookup). On the other hand, if you're moving hookups such as electric, gas, or water, then you most assuredly do need a permit. And increasingly today cities are restricting the ability of the homeowner to do such work himself or herself, and are instead requiring that professionals do it. The easiest thing to do is simply to call your city building department. (You can do this anonymously.) Describe what you're having done and ask if they require a permit. They'll be happy to tell you.

Have I checked out new appliances in magazines and online?   ☐ **yes**   ☐ **no**

Don't make the mistake of deciding what appliance to get without first checking to see what's out there. With the recent boom in renovations, manufacturers have introduced whole new model lines with amazing features, new colors, and striking designs. The various home magazines often feature these as well as give the websites of the manufacturers. Without ever leaving your home, you can find colors, styles, sizes, and prices. Magazines and online catalogs are the new, easier way to shop.

Have I checked out new appliances at stores?   ☐ **yes**   ☐ **no**

This is a fun experience that anyone considering a kitchen renovation must have. Just go to your kitchen appliance store (anyplace from Sears to a local appliance dealer) and check out the many new appliances available. You'll undoubtedly be surprised by the variety of brand names (from GE to Bosch), the enormous number of different models, and the huge price range. While only 10 years ago there were just a few different options to select from, now there are literally hundreds for each appliance type.

It's a great opportunity to fantasize about your perfect kitchen. It's also a chance to get a realistic look at what's out there and what might fit within your budget.

Have I looked for appliance manufacturers on the Internet?   ☐ yes ☐ no

Virtually all of the appliance manufacturers, from Whirl-pool to Sub-Zero, have websites. At those sites you can see which are their current models. This can be helpful in determining if a local dealer is trying to unload last year's model at this year's price. By confronting the dealer with the correct model information, you may be able to save yourself some money. The only thing that you're not likely to find on the sites is the actual pricing of models. Few manufacturers will give that to the public, preferring to rely on dealers and market pressure to determine consumer prices.

Do I know the benefits of a new dishwasher?   ☐ yes ☐ no

Before lauding the benefits of that wonderful dishwasher you've had in the kitchen for the last 12 years, check out the new models, the new *silent* models. All modern dishwashers are quieter than their predecessors. If you're willing to pay as much as a grand or more for one (say a Bosch), you can get one that's whisper quiet. And today there are stainless steel drums, food disposers built in, and precise water and drying temperature controls. In addition, there is a wide variety of colors and designs for the front. Today's dishwashers are so impressive that many high-end kitchen renovations include two of them instead of one!

Do I know the benefits of a new range/oven?   ☐ yes ☐ no

Modern range/ovens tend to reflect commercial styling. Instead of the traditional four burners, there may be six . . . or eight. Instead of "okay" heat controls, there may be precision heat monitors. Ovens often offer radiant as well as convection heating. And in some cases, microwaves are built in. Today's modern range/ovens, in fact, may not look as though they belong in a home at all, but instead with their flashy stainless steel and dark enamels appear to belong more likely in an upscale restaurant. Before opting for these, however, be sure to check how much you will actually cook in your kitchen. (See Chapter 6.) It's usually a huge waste of money to put a commercial oven/range in a kitchen for a family that always eats out.

Do I know the benefits of a new garbage disposal?   ☐ yes   ☐ no

The real problem with garbage disposals is that no one sees them, except of course, for the opening in the sink. Therefore, budget-conscious renovators are tempted simply to use the old one on the new sink. Unless the old one is almost new, that's a mistake. A new garbage disposal is unlikely to cost more than $150 plus installation. And the newer models are more powerful (one-half horsepower and up) and are more insulated, meaning that they are whisper quiet. Don't be pennywise and pound-foolish here—buy a new disposal.

Do I know the benefits of a new refrigerator?   ☐ yes   ☐ no

Refrigerators can be big-ticket items. Even a modest two-door, side-by-side model can easily cost $1000. Built-in refrigerators in the style pioneered by Sub-Zero can cost $2000 and more. (Today most refrigerator makers offer built-in models with door paneling that can match the décor of the kitchen, for a price.) Thus, the tendency by budget-conscious renovators is to do everything new in the kitchen, and then put back that tired, old refrigerator. This is probably a mistake. New models not only look better, but are also built better. Often, replacing a 10-year-old model will pay for itself in just 3 or 4 years with its energy savings. A wise idea is to consider the refrigerator as part of the overall kitchen renovation. Perhaps you can create deeper cabinets to avoid that pushed out look that many refrigerators offer. A refrigerator that matches the cabinets both in appearance and in depth is a real asset to a kitchen.

Do I know the benefits of a new compactor?   ☐ yes   ☐ no

Many home renovators consider a trash compactor an optional item. If you have it, it's nice. If you don't, then who cares? Except that if you're trying to create a modern kitchen, be aware that today trash compactors are no longer considered optional, but are considered as necessary as a garbage disposal (which itself was considered optional about 25 years ago). Typically these compactors are concealed behind a door that matches the cabinetry of the kitchen. They don't show. But when someone walks in and says, "Where's your compactor?" you simply open the door and there is it. Pay enough to get a model that's big, quiet, and powerful.

Are there certain features I must have?   ☐ yes   ☐ no

"Know thyself." If you're doing the renovation, then do it to please you, not some imaginary person who might visit your kitchen. In spite of what's been said about buying everything new, if you have an old appliance that you like and trust, stick with it. If you want avocado green panels on your appliances (even though they went out of style 20 years ago), by all means use them. If you prefer an electric stove, though everyone urges you to buy gas because the heating is quicker, don't listen. Make a short list of features that you must have and work around it. You'll be far happier afterward that you listened to yourself.

Have I created a price comparison list?   ☐ yes   ☐ no

There's budgeting when you look at what you can afford. And then there's budgeting after you see what things cost. The trick is to get the two to match. And the first step is to create a price comparison chart for each appliance. For example, you may find that dishwashers start at around $250 on the low end and peak out at around $2500 on the high end. Create a chart showing the features of the models that you like between the two extremes and determine just what the minimum cost will be. Then see if you can afford it. If not, maybe you'll want to squeeze somewhere else to increase your dishwasher's budget.

Have I measured the space I have available?   ☐ yes   ☐ no

While appliances come in relatively standard sizes, the particular unit you may want could be wider or narrower, deeper or shallower, taller or shorter than the space you currently have allotted for it. That's not usually a problem if you're putting in a new countertop and cabinets, as long as you allow for it. The one constant with appliances is that their outside dimensions are widely available from the retailers, from their websites, and on sales brochures. It's simply a matter of being aware of the problem and then avoiding it.

Have I added in the cost of delivery and installation?   ☐ **yes**   ☐ **no**

Many people simply assume that appliance delivery is part of the purchase price. Sometimes it is. But very often it is not. Be sure to determine what the charge is for getting it to your home. Then keep in mind that typically it will arrive in a large, brown cardboard box, and it's up to you to get it installed. Be sure to arrange to have someone competent handle the installation and to budget the costs for that. Installation charges for most appliances are not very high, and the general contractor you're using may be willing to absorb them.

Will I install the appliances myself?   ☐ **yes**   ☐ **no**

Some appliances are very easy to install. A countertop stove, for example, may simply plug into a socket and then drop into its slot. What could be easier (assuming that all measurements are correct!)? A dishwasher, on the other hand, usually must be adjusted to fit into its slot, and then the hot water (it doesn't use cold water) and drain (including air vent) must be installed. If you haven't done it before and don't know how, this can be quite challenging. Although most dishwashers come with detailed instructions, if you must put in a new water tap, and install the drain to the garbage disposal, and put the vent into the sink, you could end up spending days at the task, at the end only to find that it leaks! My suggestion is to pop for the $150 or so that a plumber will charge to do the work.

Are the appliances I want readily available?   ☐ **yes**   ☐ **no**

We all want what we want when we want it. But manufacturers are driven by different considerations. Production of any given unit is limited. It may be many weeks or months until just the one you want is available in your area. Your alternatives are to check out other sources (retailers, manufacturers, discounters, and so on), to wait, or to select a more readily available alternative. The mistake is to assume that the appliance is available. The better move is to put your order in long in advance of when you want delivery.

Questions to Ask Your Appliance Seller

What are the exact dimensions?
☐ yes   ☐ no

The salesperson may not know, but should be able to find out. Be wary if you are simply told a series of dimensions (height, depth, width). It's much better if you actually see the dimensions written out on a brochure from the manufacturer. That way there's far less opportunity for a mistake to enter in during the communication. If you are still unsure after talking with the retailer, contact the manufacturer directly by phone or email. Almost all will be delighted to send you brochures including accurate dimensions. This is nothing to guess over. What are you going to do if your countertop is in and you discover that your cabinets are an inch too narrow to accommodate your new appliance?

How energy efficient are they?
☐ yes   ☐ no

We live in an age of high energy costs. Thus, the energy efficiency of the appliances in your kitchen is an issue. The difference between "dirty" and efficient appliances can be as much as $50 a month or more. Over 10 years, that can add up to $6000 or more, a sizeable chunk of money. And that's before consideration of the energy conservation issue itself. Today, all appliances are rated as to their efficiency. However, the rating system does leave much to be desired. Usually, it will show the typical range of efficiency for the type of appliance and where this unit fits in. If you go with the lowest possible rating, then you're fairly assured that your unit is efficient. Some units also carry a special energy-efficient designation that helps identify them.

What are their capacities?

☐ **yes**   ☐ **no**

A super powerful dishwasher may be okay, but not if it only can handle five dishes at a time. A high-efficiency refrigerator is nice, but not if it's only 12 cubic feet. (Most people consider 20 cubic feet minimum.) Capacities should be important to you, and your salesperson should be able to laud the size of the unit you're considering. But use your common sense, too. I always get a kick out of the creative salesperson who shows a dishwasher with a tiny tub, but then points out how many more dishes can be arranged in it because the racks are built more efficiently. Maybe. But maybe simply having a bigger tub would be easier.

How loud are they?

☐ **yes**   ☐ **no**

Today, almost all appliances are also rated in terms of the noise they generate. However, the ratings can be difficult to interpret. How much quieter, for example, is "whisper" when compared to "super silent?" Often the ratings are subjective, not objective. Find out if the manufacturer rates the appliance by the number of decibels it produces at a given distance. For example, 80 decibels at 5 feet could be like a jet plane traveling overhead. Ten decibels at 5 feet would be far better. Go for the lowest decibel rating, if you can find one. Also check the distance of the measurement. The closer (as well as lower) the rating is to the machine, the better.

What types of hookups do they require?

☐ **yes**   ☐ **no**

You really need to know this in advance so that you can arrange to have the necessary hookups available. Don't assume that all electric appliances take 110 volts. Dishwashers and compactors typically do. But stoves and ovens usually require 220 volts. (It requires a rewiring to increase the voltage to a site.) Similarly, you may need hot water for a dishwasher and cold water for a refrigerator's icemaker. If you don't check this out, you could be in for a very big and expensive surprise later on.

Do you have a report on the incidence of problems and repairs?   ☐ yes   ☐ no

We've all seen the ads for the Maytag repairman sleeping on the job because his appliances have so few repair calls. That may very well be the case. But it would be much nicer to have some solid information showing how many reports of problems there are per thousand units, how severe those problems were, and how often the repairs were made under warranty without cost to the consumer. All manufacturers maintain such information, but many simply will not release it. Try to find out the real statistics from the dealer, or directly from the manufacturer. Also check out the ratings that *Consumer Reports* magazine offers.

What is the warranty period?   ☐ yes   ☐ no

Obviously, the longer the warranty lasts, the better. With regard to appliances, I would say that an absolute minimum would be one year for parts and labor. Since these are used relatively infrequently, a 90-day warranty may be useless. A word about buying extended warranties. Some people swear by them. However, if you were to buy extended warranties for all your appliances, chances are it would cost you as much as to replace any individual piece. My feeling is that it's best to self-insure. If something goes out after the warranty period, I'll take care of it myself. If only one unit goes out, I'm probably even. If none goes out, I may be well ahead. Quite frankly, most appliances these days are very well built. I've found that if they don't crash in the first year, they'll probably go on ticking for a very long time.

Who handles warranty repairs?   ☐ yes   ☐ no

Don't assume it's the store where you're buying the appliance that will do any repairs. It may very well not be. Rather, the manufacturer may have contracted with a small appliance dealer in a distant city to handle repairs in your area. This means that there could be delays in getting service. Remember, with a kitchen appliance you aren't likely to bring the item back into a store. Every call is a visit to your house. If the manufacturer doesn't have warranty service available near where you live, it might be a good reason to choose a different manufacturer who does.

What is the price?   ☐ **yes**   ☐ **no**

Don't assume that the price is what the sticker on the appliance says. It might be less . . . or more. Finding the price on an appliance actually can be much more difficult than finding the price on a new car, where federal law mandates stickers showing manufacturer's prices. Since manufacturers often won't release their MSRPs, sometimes the best thing to do is to price shop different dealers. The hard part, of course, is finding two dealers in close proximity who carry the exact same units.

Will you give me a discount?   ☐ **yes**   ☐ **no**

We live in an extremely competitive environment where almost no one pays full retail. Discounting is the rule, not the exception. I often walk into an appliance store and before even selecting the item I'm interested in, I will ask, "How big a discount are you offering today?" Sometimes the answer will be a negative, but more than likely the salesperson will say, "We'll take good care of you, depending on what you buy." The implication, of course, is that the higher the price, the deeper the discount. Keep in mind that some stores will give you an automatic discount if you open one of their credit card accounts. Others have weekly or monthly sales. If you have time, you might watch their sales over a period of four to six months to see if they feature just the appliance you want deeply discounted.

Can you give me the color I want?   ☐ **yes**   ☐ **no**

Everything's perfect–the right appliances, they fit, they can be delivered on time, and cost and installation are within budget. But they don't come in quite the right color. Or the right color just doesn't happen to be available for four months. Keep in mind that color is as critical a feature as size, noise, or even price. If you can't get the right color, then for practical purposes you don't have a fit. If you opt to go with a different color, will it work with the cabinets, countertops, and kitchen color you've chosen? Might it not be better to go with a different manufacturer? Or search around for a different dealer who might have a better selection?

Do you deliver?   ☐ yes   ☐ no

If they do, then the next question should be, "How much do you charge?" Some retailers are quite rigid. They charge $35 to deliver per item purchased. Buy 1 and it's $35. But 10 and it's $350. Of course, that makes no sense since it's only one delivery whether it's 1 or 10 items. Try to negotiate the price of delivery if you're buying a whole kitchen's worth of appliances. For the profit the dealer's making, it ought to throw in free delivery. But if not, there should be, at most, one minimal charge. Be sure that delivery can be made on the exact day (or sooner) that you'll need the appliances.

Questions to Ask Your Contractor

Will you handle new hookups?   ☐ yes   ☐ no

Most general contractors will not. Instead they will sub it out to plumbers, electricians, or whatever. And they'll add on a management charge for doing this. You can often save a considerable sum (10 to 30 percent of the hookup costs) simply by telling the contractor that you'll sub it out yourself. You can even ask the GC who his or her favorite plumber and electrician are. Of course, be sure to get several bids. Changing hookups can be no small thing. You could easily spend $5000 or 10,000 moving around water, drain, and electricity.

Will you handle appliance installation?   ☐ yes   ☐ no

Most general contractors will do this, provided that no specialized work is involved. They should install the stove and oven without blinking an eye. Moving in a refrigerator is something they will probably do as a favor.

Hooking up a trash compactor is a bother, but they'll do it. But many draw the line when it comes to a dishwasher and disposal. They don't want to get involved with plumbing and the problems that it can cause. Thus, you might get your GC to handle almost all of your installation and only have to call in a plumber (or electrician) for a couple of items.

Are there particular brands that you recommend?   ☐ yes   ☐ no

A renovation contractor who remodels homes day in and day out will probably have seen most brands. He or she will have an opinion on which are the easiest to install and which, if any, don't work right out of the box. Be sure to listen, but take what the contractor says with a grain of salt. Chances are that he or she will have no real evidence to support how well the appliances work over the long haul. Remember, complaints about breakdowns go to the manufacturer, not the installer or GC.

Are there any problems with the appliances I've chosen?   ☐ yes   ☐ no

If you don't ask, you may not find out. Has the builder had problems installing any of the appliances (model or manufacturer) that you're buying? If so, what are they? Is it a big enough problem to make you reconsider your purchase?

Can you get me a deal on appliances?   ☐ yes   ☐ no

There are builder's prices on almost anything that goes into a house. With a contractor's license, a renovator can go to almost any building supply store and demand and get sometimes hefty discounts. Ask your general contractor if he or she will do this for you as a favor. Many find it a bother, but will agree. Then have them go to the store where you've picked out the appliances you want and see if they can get a discount for you. Keep in mind, this only works *before* you actually make the purchase. Once you've bought the appliance(s) on your own, don't expect the contractor to be able to go into the store and get some sort of a discount.

How long will it take to install?   ☐ yes   ☐ no

Since installing appliances is often the last step in the renovation process (with the possible exception of painting),
you'll want to know how long installation will take
because it will influence how soon you'll be able to get
into that kitchen and start using it. For some things, such
as a stove or oven, the contractor may say, "About an
hour or so." For others, such as a dishwasher, particularly
where there are complications, the answer may be a day
or more. Generally speaking, however, installing appliances is one of the quickest procedures in renovating.

11
Installing Bathroom Fixtures

Questions to Ask Yourself

Will new fixtures fit in my bathroom?

☐ yes ☐ no

Don't assume that anything new will fit. It's rare that a new toilet's footprint will match that footprint of the old toilet, meaning that you may need to put in new flooring. A new sink will almost never fit in the space left by an old sink, which means installing a new countertop. Tubs and showers come in all sorts of sizes and shapes that almost certainly will have different profiles from what you currently have. Be sure to obtain both the exact old measurements as well as the new ones. And if you must make an assumption, assume that the new fixture simply won't fit.

Will I do the installation myself?

☐ yes ☐ no

You certainly can, and in most situations it's not hard. It does, however, require that you talk with a plumber or read up on how it's done. Keep in mind, however, that some of the fixtures are very heavy, such as the toilet. And in order to install it correctly, you'll have to lift it straight up and place it straight down. If you can't do this yourself, be sure you have a hefty helper. Also, placing showers and tubs in the bathroom can be tricky because of their large size. Sometimes it's necessary to tear out a wall to get them in! If you're totally new to this, you may want to consider having a pro do it for you.

Do I have drain and water hookups where needed?   ☐ yes   ☐ no

You may begin to put a new tub in where the old one was
and discover that the drains don't line up. Or you may try
putting a shower on a wall different from where the current shower is, but there are no hot and cold water lines
there. Or your new flooring raises the level of the toilet so
it no longer fits on its flange. These, unfortunately, are
some of the common problems that occur when trying to
install bathroom fixtures. The answer to them is to take
precise measurements. However, keep in mind that when
dealing with bathroom fixtures, you're not dealing with
simple boxes. Often there are round corners and unusual
shapes. Be sure to double and triple check that your measurements are accurate.

How much will it cost to install new hookups?   ☐ yes   ☐ no

It can be enormously expensive. If you need to move the
toilet drain over just six inches, it could mean cutting into
a slab of concrete (assuming you're not on a raised floor)
and relocating a line. To move a shower from one side of
the bathroom to the other probably means completely
relocating vents, which if you have a two-story house,
may be extremely difficult. Just getting hot and cold water
lines into a wall where a shower will go can require going
through the ceiling or basement and cutting up walls that
otherwise would not need to be touched. Before deciding
to move forward on a renovation project involving new
hookups, be sure to find out the cost of those hookups.
You just might find that it's far easier and less expensive to
leave things where they are!

Do I need a special permit?   ☐ yes   ☐ no

Any time you move a plumbing line, whether it be potable
water, sanitary drain, or vent, you need a permit. Your
city's building department will want to see that what
you've done is up to current building code standards. This
is for your own health and safety. Improperly hooked-up
plumbing could mean the mixing of sewerage with potable water resulting in terrible diseases. On the other
hand, many times plumbers who are simply replacing one

toilet with another or trading out sinks won't bother with the permit. Presumably they know what they're doing. Nevertheless, it won't hurt to call the building department to ask just what they require permits for.

Can I install a toilet?   ☐ **yes**   ☐ **no**

A toilet is installed once the final floor is finished (unless you plan to tile right up to the edge of the toilet, which is not recommended). A flange made out of metal or plastic comes up from a four-inch drain and attaches to the sub-floor. A wax seal goes onto the flange (or the toilet) and then the fixture is placed down on the flange. Pressure causes the wax to spread, forming a (hopefully) perfect seal. A few screws around the toilet hold it in place, and hooking it up to the cold water line finishes the installation. If everything fits, you can hook up a toilet in just a few minutes. The usual way to check is to flush it several times to see if any water leaks out at the base. If none does, and the water line to the tank doesn't leak, the installation is probably correct. Have a plumber check it to be sure.

Can I install a sink?   ☐ **yes**   ☐ **no**

Sinks fit either over the countertop or flush with it using a ring, or sometimes, special hooks from underneath. Usually, the fittings necessary to install the sink will come with it. It's a good idea to put the hardware (faucet, drain, and so on) on the sink *before* attempting installation, as they're difficult to get to afterward. For flush installation, often a bead of silicone sealant is all that's necessary to hold the sink in place. For freestanding sinks, it's usually necessary to drill screws into the back wall and affix it using them. Be sure you drill into studs, or prepare the wall properly lest the sink fall off! Freestanding sinks use a pedestal through which the drain and sometimes the water supply are fitted. Have a plumber help with the more difficult installations.

Can I install a mirror?   ☐ **yes**   ☐ **no**

Bathroom mirrors are either glued to walls or have special hooks that attach them to the wallboard, and in some cases to the studs behind. The installation is not difficult, but it is made tricky by the cumbersome size and weight of many mirrors. If the mirror is large, be sure to have help. The biggest concern is that you'll accidentally scratch or break the mirror surface, which means going out and buying another mirror. Also, if you get a break, be sure to watch out for the glass edges, which can be very sharp and dangerous. Read up in a home renovation book on how to install mirrors properly before attempting it.

Can I install a shower/tub?   ☐ yes   ☐ no

As noted earlier, the biggest concern is that the drains won't line up. Other than that, it's a matter of getting it into the small confines of the bathroom and moving it into place. Most retrofit shower/tub combinations come in sections for easier installation. Lining up the water connections shouldn't be difficult, as there's usually some room to play. For fiberglass showers, it's usually just a matter of drilling the water supply holes where you want them. You may end up feeling like a contortionist trying to get this to fit into place, but with patience and a little help, it's not really all that difficult.

Can I install a shower/tub glass door?   ☐ yes   ☐ no

Installing a glass door is a great starter project to see how well you like renovation work. The frame for the glass door sits on the edge of the tub and is held in place by silicone sealant. The edges are held to the walls by screws. When drilling into tile, use care not to break the tile. (A small, high-quality masonry drill usually does the trick.) Once the frame is in place, the glass doors can be hung. Most glass tub/shower doors allow you some movement to accommodate a variety of wall widths. Be sure that you are careful when hanging the doors. You don't want them to hit something and break. (You should, of course, only use safety glass in a bathroom.)

Can I install a heater/towel warmer?   ☐ yes   ☐ no

These usually have only two kinds of installation—on top of the wall and within the wall. On top of the wall is the easiest since it simply means screwing the appliance to something solid, like a stud. (Molly-bolt-type screws will also work on sheet rock. Check with your building department for what they'll allow.) The wiring connection should be done by an electrician, unless you're competent to handle it yourself. Needless to say, all power should be off when installing. Be sure that the heater or towel warmer isn't where towels or toilet paper or other flammables are likely to brush against it.

Have I checked out new fixtures in magazines and on the Internet?

☐ yes   ☐ no

If you haven't looked at new bathroom fixtures in the last five years, be prepared for a shock. They now come in all sizes, shapes, colors, and materials. You can get Lucite toilet seats and glass sinks. Faucets are not only made from brass, but from gold, copper, nickel, and a host of other metals. You can buy a toilet that's a combination bidet and tush warmer! Have fun by checking these out in home and bath magazines. There are a host of them on every newsstand. Then go to the websites of the manufacturers for more detailed pictures and virtual tours of model bathrooms. It's a wonderful and pleasant way to see what your options are.

Have I checked out new fixtures at stores and model homes?

☐ yes   ☐ no

Plumbing supply stores usually offer model bathrooms. These are typically set up using the fixtures sold by the store. By seeing them in actual bathroom settings, you can get a better idea of how they'll look in your home. Also, whenever you get a chance, check out any local model homes that contractors have put up. These days, bathrooms are a big part of selling the home. The new baths are elaborate, sometimes elegant. You can get all sorts of wonderful renovation ideas simply by spending some weekends checking out the new home models in your area.

Have I checked out less expensive alternatives?

☐ yes   ☐ no

Whether you're leaning toward Kohler, Price-Pfister, Moen, Delta (to name some of the more popular brands), or other lines, keep in mind that that there's a huge range of price. You can just as easily spend $1,000 on a faucet as

$100. Some of the more upscale lines include gold, silver, and platinum plating that send prices into the stratosphere. However, if you're on a budget, it's nice to know that less expensive alternatives exist for all bathroom fixtures. However, don't be penny-wise and pound-foolish. Below a certain point, quality drops off. For example, if you're getting a porcelain sink, be sure it's solid ceramic, not thin metal overlaid with porcelain. It's a mistake to trade price for quality, as poor quality always shows to those who know what to look for.

Are there certain features that I must have?   ☐ yes   ☐ no

You may want a sink faucet with old-fashioned circular spigots, or a built-in shower that doesn't need a door. Or a toilet that's purple. Or whatever. I can assure you that almost certainly whatever your fancy, it's out there, for a price. If you have definite wants, then by all means keep looking until you get them satisfied. It may take a little longer and cost a little more, but if you get exactly the fixtures you're looking for, you'll be far happier with the way your bathroom turns out.

Have I created a price-comparison list?   ☐ yes   ☐ no

As always, don't commit to particular fixtures until you know how they stack up against the competition. Your comparison list may take into account models within a brand as well as many different brands. Just be sure that you compare apples with apples and not with oranges. For example, you may be putting in a whirlpool tub and need a Roman-style spigot and faucets for it. Some may only cost $300, but others may cost $1000. In addition to appearance, check for features. For example, the lower-priced unit may only offer a quarter-inch water line, which means it will take 20 minutes to fill the tub. The larger unit could offer a half-inch or three-quarter-inch line, which could fill the tub in 5 minutes or less. You may pay less initially for the smaller capacity, but you'll pay with regret every time you use the tub. Get capacities, colors, styles, materials, sizes, and all other features when you comparison shop.

Have I added in the cost of installation?

☐ yes   ☐ no

If you're doing it yourself (as indicated by the questions above), then your installation costs will be low, basically just parts (and band aids, as the case may be!). On the other hand, if you're going to have the fixtures professionally installed, be sure that you get an accurate estimate from a plumber. And be sure that the plumber sees or at least is familiar with what you want installed. Some items take a lot more time and are far trickier to install than others, and this will affect the bid.

What is the maximum price I am willing to pay for new fixtures?

☐ yes   ☐ no

It's common practice to set a price ceiling. However, it's just as common to keep moving that ceiling upward as we get more educated about what's available out there and how much it costs. Try not to be inflexible. And inure yourself against sticker-shock. Bathroom fixtures are expensive and getting more so every day. Perhaps, after the current renovation boom ends, prices will come down. But for now, they're only going up. You'll want to go back to your pencil and calculator many times before you come up with a final figure for how much you'll be willing to pay (or borrow) to finish your renovation. And it's far better that you do this before you get started, than when you're halfway through the project.

Are the fixtures I want available?

☐ yes   ☐ no

There might be a shipping strike. The factory could have shut down. It might be last year's model and out of stock. The local dealer just sold his or her last one, and it will be a month before the next shipment arrives. This is a common headache with regard to buying any fixtures for the bathroom. It's so common, in fact, that the first question some homeowners ask is, "Is it available?" If it's not, they don't want to see any more of it, even if it's billed as a real bargain. Remember, it's not what you can buy for the money that counts–it's what actually gets delivered.

Is there an additional cost for shipping?   ☐ yes   ☐ no

Some items, such as a sink or toilet, can be hauled in the back of your car or in a pickup truck. Other items, such as a large tub/shower enclosure, are better delivered. Find out what delivery charges are. As with most other building supplies, there's a wide range here. It could be only $50 to bring everything over to your house. Or there could be a $100-per-item charge. It's important to know costs when comparison shopping, particularly for a dealer. If the prices are the same and one dealer will deliver for free while the other charges, you know where to make your purchase.

Questions to Ask Your Bathroom Fixture Seller

What are the exact dimensions?   ☐ yes   ☐ no

You need two sets of dimensions–the space available in your bathroom, and how much room the fixtures require. Sometimes this can be tricky. For example, while most sinks have a standard width for faucets, some can vary. Be sure that the faucets you buy will fit the sink that you have. Similarly, shower stalls come in some standard widths, but there are exceptions. When it comes to measurements, never assume. Always measure, and do it twice!

How are they installed?   ☐ yes   ☐ no

If you're planning on doing it yourself, you can often get some very important help from the salesperson. He or she can show you exactly how the installation is carried out. For example, you will want to install faucets on a sink before installing the sink, to make the process much easier. Fiberglass shower stalls come with a template to help you locate where faucets and showerheads should go. The sales person may be able to tell you in a few quick sentences exactly how it's done. On the other hand, the installation instructions that come with the fixture may be short and confusing.

Do they require any special hookups? ☐ **yes** ☐ **no**

A toilet that blows hot air will require both a cold water *and* an electric hookup. A towel warmer may require a separate 110-volt or 220-volt connection. A spa may require three-quarter-inch copper piping to carry the added water flow required to fill it quickly, instead of the usual half-inch copper piping. Be sure to ask what special hookups are required. The salesperson may surprise you with what you need, to the point where you may actually decide not to make the purchase! Or to purchase a different and easier-to-connect fixture.

What is the warranty period? ☐ **yes** ☐ **no**

Warranty periods vary, and some are determined by who does the installation. If you install the product yourself, you may shorten the warranty period. Don't take the salesperson's word for this. Ask to see the warranty documentation. Typically, it will be in a book listing the various products. With bathroom fixtures, one of the biggest problems is that they could arrive broken or chipped. In that case, you want to be assured that the retailer will exchange them for good fixtures, no questions asked.

Will you give me a discount? ☐ **yes** ☐ **no**

It never hurts to ask for a discount. Some stores offer discounts as a standard procedure, but you must ask for them. Others never offer discounts. Sometimes, with large suppliers, if you'll take out one of their credit cards and charge the purchase, you can get a 10-percent discount. Others will discount fixtures if you buy all of them at the same store. Look especially for closeout items–often the last of a manufacturer's model. Sometimes the discounts on these can be as much as 50 percent!

Can you give me the color I want? ☐ **yes** ☐ **no**

Never assume that you'll be able to get the color you want. The old rule is that every color will be in stock, except yours. And don't assume that the fixture inside the box is the right color regardless of what it says on the outside of the box. Always check first. Finally, be sure you know what color you're actually getting. The difference between almond and white can be subtle when you're checking out a fixture under a store's fluorescent lighting. I once installed an almond sink, only to discover when the lighting was better that it was cream colored!

Do you deliver?   ☐ yes   ☐ no

You can easily haul small fixtures with you. But larger ones require delivery. Yet some building supply stores simply won't deliver anything. Others charge a hefty fee for it. Be especially careful if you live more than 10 miles from the store, as the delivery charges can mount very rapidly. I once was having a fiberglass shower stall delivered to a mountain home more than 60 miles away from the store where I bought it. The delivery charges were more than the stall itself!

Questions to Ask Your Contractor

Will you handle new hookups?   ☐ yes   ☐ no

If the general contractor you have doing the work handles this, you can probably get a good price on it. However, if the GC intends to sub it out to a plumber or electrician, you might be better off doing the subbing yourself. That way you can negotiate directly with the plumber or electrician over the best price. And you can always consider doing it yourself.

Will you handle fixture installation?   ☐ yes   ☐ no

Some contractors will install bathroom cabinets and countertops, but won't put in the sink. Others will do the whole job. It's usually much better if the person handling the tiling, for example, puts in the tub, shower, and sink. These fixtures go in when the tiling is done, and to do them afterward can sometimes make for an awkward fit.

Can you get me a deal on fixtures? ☐ yes ☐ no

Don't overlook the contractor's discount. It can be anywhere from 5 to 40 percent. If you're doing the installation yourself, the contractor may be more than happy to
help you out by passing along his or her savings. But
don't expect the contractor to take the time to go down to
the building supply store, help you pick out the fixture,
and then cart it home for you. Time is money, and contractors will charge for all the time they spend. On the
other hand, if it's simply making a call to a building supply store to authorize your making a purchase on the contractor's account, that's another matter.

How long will it take to install? ☐ yes ☐ no

Get a good time frame. Most fixtures can be installed
within a couple of hours. The exceptions are when there
are problems getting them in. Fitting a one-piece tub/
shower enclosure into a small bathroom could take days
and could require ripping out walls. Be sure that you get
a solid estimate from your contractor.

Are there any problems with the fixtures I've chosen? ☐ yes ☐ no

The contractor may have had previous experience with
the product and may know that it's difficult to install. Or
that over time it gives owners problems. This is valuable
information that may not be volunteered, unless you ask.

12
Installing Electrical Fixtures

Questions to Ask Yourself

Can I do the work myself?

☐ yes ☐ no

The answer is maybe. Most electrical work requires a permit, and some building departments will only allow professionals to do the work. Other building departments will allow you, as an owner, to do electrical work, but only if you agree to live in the property for a period of time, say six months or a year. In any event, you should *not* do electrical work unless you are fully qualified and even then, you should have it checked by a professional electrician. Be sure that whenever you do any electrical work the *power is off*!

Can I do simple installations?

☐ yes ☐ no

It depends on what constitutes "simple." Screwing in a light bulb is simple. Replacing a wired-in fixture is also fairly simple, and many home renovators can do that themselves. But if you get the wires crossed or don't insulate them properly, you can cause a short, and possibly, a fire. Read the previous question. Only do electrical work of any kind if you're fully qualified to do so. Otherwise, it pays to hire an electrician, no matter how expensive that may be.

Do I want new electrical fixtures? ☐ yes ☐ no

Almost certainly, yes, you will want new electrical fixtures. Some home renovators make the mistake of thinking that they can scrimp and save on their light fixtures. They put in a whole new kitchen or bath, and then try to retain the old lighting. That's almost as bad as putting in new cabinets and then not painting the kitchen. Lighting is crucial not only in making it easier to use the new work areas, but also in presentation. Today, the rule is new lighting fixtures, new wall switches, and even new wall plugs. And sometimes you'll want to put these in throughout the house, even though you're only renovating one small area.

How much will it cost to install new electrical fixtures? ☐ yes ☐ no

Be prepared for sticker shock. Ceiling and wall lights, the kind you simply replace, cost anywhere from under $20 to well over $1000, but the installation is virtually nothing. Recessed lighting only costs about $50 per light, but installation can easily run hundreds per fixture and more. And if you have to drop down a ceiling and create new hookups, add many thousands more. In short, plan ahead with your electrical fixture needs. Check out what you want, what it will cost, and how much installation will be. And do this *before* you create your final budget.

Do I need to cut holes in ceilings or walls? ☐ yes ☐ no

Anytime that you need to put a light fixture where there wasn't one before, count on cutting holes. It might only be a small hole to house an electrical box. Or it could be a big hole for a recessed light. However, unless you cut very carefully so that there's no extra space around the new box, and unless the new fixture completely covers the hole, be prepared to retexture and repaint the wall. This is why it pays to look for light fixtures that are *big*!

Do I need to string new wiring? ☐ yes ☐ no

My wife likes to look at a room and say something such as, "I'd like a light fixture at that point in the ceiling, two wall sconces over there, and a dimmer switch in the corner." Of course, my stomach is sinking as I think about how much it will cost to wire all of this. Whenever you put an electrical fixture in a location where there isn't one already, you're going to have to bring wiring to it. If it's in a ceiling and there's an attic or crawlspace, then the work is fairly easy. But if it's in a wall, floor, or ceiling with no attic above, it can be a nightmare. Call in an electrician and hear the bad news.

Can my existing circuit breaker panel handle the fixtures? ☐ yes ☐ no

It depends on when your home was built. Modern homes built in the last 25 years tend to have much larger circuit breaker panels, 200 amps and higher. Older homes tend to have smaller panels, 100 amps or less. The more amps, the more circuits the panel can hold. You'll need to check with an electrician to see whether your panel can take extra circuits, or if you're lucky, if your existing circuits can handle extra light fixtures. If your home is very old and still uses fuses, you may find out that the building department will require you to rip out the fuse box and replace it with a circuit breaker panel, if you do any renovation work.

Is there a maximum wattage I can get for the new fixtures? ☐ yes ☐ no

If you're using an existing circuit, you may be limited to the size of the electrical fixture it can handle. You may want to get fixtures whose total wattage is only, say 600 watts (which isn't much for four fixtures). In other cases, if your application is in or on ceilings or walls, there may be a maximum wattage that the base you're installing can handle. Often this is very low, 100 or even just 60 watts. If that's the case, you'll need to purchase fixtures accordingly. Keep in mind that some fixtures look good with low-watt bulbs, while others only look good with megawatt bulbs. Most fixtures will state the maximum wattage they can handle.

Do I want incandescent or fluorescent fixtures? ☐ yes ☐ no

Most people, once they understand the difference, opt for incandescent fixtures, particularly the kinds that use the many new types of high-efficiency bulbs. The reason is the quality of light. Incandescent fixtures give off a yellow light that is very pleasing, some might say soothing. Most fluorescent fixtures give off a green light. You might not think it's green, because your brain automatically processes the light source and tries to turn it into white light. But a part of you still knows. And if it's in a kitchen, it can mean that for just a moment that cheese will look green! Of course, per-watt fluorescent fixtures tend to give the most light. That's why many building departments mandate their use in bathrooms. One compromise is to have both kinds of lighting. That way you can decide whether you want a more efficient, or a more pleasant lighting appearance in a room.

Have I checked out new electrical fixtures in magazines?

☐ yes   ☐ no

A whole new world of electrical fixtures has emerged from the wave of renovations that has swept the country over the last few years. If you want to see quickly what's hot, just pick up any of the many home and redecorating magazines that are on the newsstands. They tend to feature the latest and the most artistic fixtures (and sometimes the most bizarre!). Be sure to check out lights attached to fans as well as wall lights, which are now in vogue. Usually magazines list websites of lighting manufacturers featured on their pages. Check them out for more ideas, as well as to find local dealers.

Have I checked out new electrical fixtures at stores?

☐ yes   ☐ no

Home Depot, Lowes, Do It Center, and other major building supply stores usually have an entire electrical fixture department. They have all of the products they carry hanging from the ceiling or displayed on the wall, with lights turned on. It's a great opportunity to see up close what a fixture will look like. However, there are also many local and regional stores devoted exclusively to lighting fixtures. Check the yellow pages. Often, these independent stores will have the highest prices (on unique fixtures) as well as some of the lowest prices (on more common fixtures).

Do I know the range of cost for each electrical fixture? ☐ yes ☐ no

When you're renovating, the worst thing you can do is to pop into a store, look at a lighting fixture, and decide on the spot that you must have it. Of course, your searching is done. But you may find that you're paying $500 for a fixture while a similar one in a different store only costs $150. Don't fall in love with any lighting fixtures until you've seen the broad spectrum of what's out there. As in almost no other area, the variety here is simply enormous, and the price range is wide.

Have I created a price-comparison list? ☐ yes ☐ no

Don't try to keep track of the different lighting fixtures in your head. A better way is to create a list. If possible, include the size and a picture of the fixture so that you can instantly remember which one it is. Of course, include the price. And put all the fixtures you will want to buy for each room on separate lists. The reason is that while an eclectic approach to lighting fixtures is not bad, a more sensible approach is to get fixtures that complement each other, at least by room. Don't forget to include fans, and recessed and any track lighting you may want. Often, comparing different types of lighting (from recessed to flush mount) can be very helpful in finding a way to stay on budget.

Have I added in the cost of installation? ☐ yes ☐ no

It's not what you pay for the light fixture that counts. It's what you pay to have the light fixture in your home, and that includes installation. For replacing surface-mounted fixtures, as noted, the cost is minimal. But start moving into the realm of built-in lighting, especially recessed lights, and the installation soon far exceeds the cost of the fixture itself. When preparing a comparison list, be sure it includes the cost of installation.

What is the maximum price I am willing to pay for new electrical fixtures? ☐ yes ☐ no

You have a budget, right? You're not going to go over it, right! Wrong! Lighting fixtures is not an area where you will want to scrimp and save. Rather, lighting is very important. It, so to speak, puts everything else you renovate in the proper light! Then there's the matter of putting in décor switches and plugs to modernize your home. When you're creating your renovation budget, don't simply put down a low number for lighting fixtures. Rather, find out what you need, what things cost, and then adjust your thinking from there. You may find that you're spending much more than anticipated on your lighting bill.

Are they available?   ☐ yes   ☐ no

You walk into a building supply or lighting store and see just the fixture you want. You check the price, it's within budget, so you call the salesperson over and say that you want one of those. But you're told that they're all sold out. It'll take three months to get the next batch in. What can you do? Of course, you can wait. Or you can find out the manufacturer, check its website, and locate other dealers who might have the fixture in stock. You can even query the manufacturer about selling directly to you. Keep in mind, however, that the price is likely to be the same. Manufacturers who undercut their own retailers are just cutting their own throats. Few will do it.

Is there an additional cost for shipping?   ☐ yes   ☐ no

Since you can usually take most lighting fixtures with you, a shipping cost usually only applies if you're getting delivery from the plant or from a retailer some distance away. If there is a cost, be sure that you add it to your comparison chart.

Questions to Ask Your Electrical Fixture Seller

What are the exact dimensions?   ☐ yes   ☐ no

Be sure you know the footprint that the electrical fixture, box, plate, or other appliance will take. When building new, this is not crucial. But when you're renovating, you already have something that you're replacing. If the footprint for the new fixture is different, especially if it is smaller, it could require anything from simple repainting to replastering to new hookups. Check the box. Often there is a template included that will not only give the exact dimensions, but also a sketch of exactly how much space it will take.

What is their wattage/amperage? ☐ **yes** ☐ **no**

You will need to know this for different applications. If your circuit's limit is 600 watts and the fixture uses 1000 watts, you've got a problem. You have to get either a lower-wattage fixture or increase the capacity of the circuit, which usually means heavier wires, circuit breaker, boxes, and switches. (Amperage is commonly used in measuring motors and heavier-duty equipment.) Circuit breakers are all rated in amps, typically from 10 to 50 or higher.

What is the warranty period? ☐ **yes** ☐ **no**

Typically, you'll get 90 days to a year on parts and labor. However, with electrical fixtures, there's rarely an issue over whether or not they work. Rather, it's an issue if a glass fixture cover is broken right out of the box or if parts are missing. Be sure that the retailer is willing to take the fixture back without question for at least 30 days. And keep track of the 30 days. With renovations, it's often the case (particularly when there's a sale) that you'll buy materials well in advance of when you'll need them. If the end of those 30 days is fast approaching, at the least take the fixture out of the box and check it out. Especially with glass fixtures, the rate for breakage in transit is sometimes as high as 15 percent!

Will you give me a discount? ☐ **yes** ☐ **no**

If you're buying just one electrical fixture, it's unlikely that the dealer will offer a discount. But if you're buying a household's worth, particularly if you're also buying cabinets, countertops, paint, and so on, it's a different story. Even many large building supply stores will be hard-pressed not to give you an overall discount on everything you buy, provided it is purchased within a limited window of time. And don't forget to check for weekly sales. Ask a salesperson if he or she knows when the item you want will next go on sale. If it's a month away, you may want to wait in order to save yourself some money.

Can you give me the color and style I want?   ☐ yes   ☐ no

Color and style can be the most frustrating things. You've found just the light fixture you want. But it's only available in antique bronze, yet you want it in a bright gold finish. Or it looks perfect, but it's a ceiling mount, and you want it to hang from a chain. If you don't find exactly what you want with lighting fixtures, it doesn't mean that it isn't out there. Check the manufacturers' websites for a far more thorough presentation of what they offer than you'll find at any one dealer. Keep in mind that often, different manufacturers will offer similar fixtures, in different styles, one of which may be perfect for you. Start early so you'll have time to look carefully.

Do you deliver?   ☐ yes   ☐ no

In many cases, this is a function of size and weight. You are usually expected to carry away smaller fixtures. Larger ones, particularly chandeliers, may be delivered. Delivery for these larger items may well be worth it, even if it costs a little extra. The reason is breakage. Anytime there's loose glass involved, as there often is with lighting fixtures, breakage happens. If you brought it home, there's always the suggestion that you accidentally broke it. If, however, it was delivered by the store, then the onus is on them.

Questions to Ask Your Contractor

Will you handle electrical hookups?   ☐ yes   ☐ no

Many times, particularly if your renovation is of a more modest nature, you may be using a handyman. He may be able to do all sorts of things. He may be the one who rips out the wall, and puts in the wall, cabinets, and sink.

And he may volunteer to handle the electrical hookups. There's nothing wrong with this, *if* he or she does it in a manner that's safe, correct, and up to building code standards. However, if the handyman is just winging it, then you should say, "No," and hire a professional to handle it.

Are you licensed to do electrical work?   ☐ yes   ☐ no

You should check to see if the person is, in fact, licensed. It's unlikely that an unlicensed person will be able to pull an electrical building permit to work on someone else's home. This may mean that the handyman is doing this without a permit. As indicated earlier, this is a no-no. If the work is done without a permit, you may have trouble when you sell the house later on. In addition, you could have trouble with your insurance company if there is an electrically caused short or fire, particularly if someone is injured.

Do I need to be the one to call in an electrician?   ☐ yes   ☐ no

Perhaps your general contractor (or handyman) can recommend one. While you can certainly find them in the yellow pages, it's often better if you can get a recommendation. Sometimes, a tile installer or a plumber will know of a good electrician and can give you his or her home phone number. Tell the electrician that you've got a small job, and ask if he or she will take it on. If the electrician works for a large company, he or she may be happy to do a small job for you. The electrician will still make good money, but he or she might cut you a break in terms of price.

Can you get me a deal on electrical fixtures?   ☐ yes   ☐ no

Electricians will certainly be able to get the standard builder's discount that's available to everyone in the industry. But it would be a rare electrician who can get you an additional discount. More likely you'll get a discount from an interior designer who has connections with manufacturers.

How long will it take to install?

☐ yes ☐ no

Once the hookups are in place, the installation is usually very quick. Chandeliers are the exception, especially elaborate glass ones that require very careful installation. Find out how long it's going to take, and make sure you allot time in your logistical planning of the renovation.

Are there any problems with the electrical fixtures I've chosen?

☐ yes ☐ no

Have the contractor open the boxes and take a look. He or she will probably say that everything looks standard. On the other hand, the contractor may hold one up and say, "What's that?" For example, I once bought a beautiful bathroom fixture for the ceiling only to discover that it was intended only for vertical wall installations. If the contractor or electrician doesn't know how to hook it up, make sure that it's not going to be a problem. You'll need to get explicit instructions, and you may even need to work with the installer to be sure that it's done correctly.

13
Painting

Questions to Ask Yourself

Can I handle the painting myself? ☐ yes ☐ no

If you want to save some money on your renovation and you're not particularly handy, this is probably the one area where you can save by doing it yourself. Of course, that assumes that you can paint! In the old days (more than 25 years ago), house painting was an art. Today, however, with rollers and synthetic bristle brushes, most people can do a fairly good job. Just be sure to buy the very best paint. The few extra dollars per gallon you spend will more than pay for itself with ease of application.

Do I need Home Owner's Association permission for colors? ☐ yes ☐ no

If you are part of an HOA, you may very well need its permission for new exterior colors for your home. Of course, inside colors are entirely up to you. Be sure to submit colors (with swatches) early enough for comment from the HOA board. In some cases, homes with strict CC&Rs (conditions, covenants, and restrictions) may also require adherence to color control. This is usually enforced by the building department or planning commission.

Have I checked with an interior designer for inside colors? ☐ yes ☐ no

Most of us are quite convinced that we are experts when it comes to color. However, you might be surprised. If you're going to spend the money to paint the interior (or exterior) of your home, why not spend a few extra dollars to get an expert's opinion on what colors will look best? Often, paint stores can provide assistance. Interior designers should also be able to give you good ideas.

Can the paint store provide me with swatches?   ☐ yes   ☐ no

Of course they can. Swatches are small patches of paper onto which colors have been painted. You can take these home and see how they'll look. The problem with them, however, is two-fold. First, they're tiny, and as a consequence, it's usually very difficult to get a good idea of how a large area of the paint will look. Second, every batch of paint is slightly different. It's unlikely that the paint you finally get will exactly match the swatch. Therefore, a better idea is to use the swatches only to get close. Then buy a quart (or pint if available) of the color and paint it onto a wall. Only then will you get a true sense of what it's going to look like.

How much will the paint cost?   ☐ yes   ☐ no

The last time I looked, a gallon of high-quality interior paint was running anywhere from $20 to $30. The difference in cost typically comes in three areas. The first is "hide"–how well the paint will hide the color underneath. A good hide means that you won't have to paint it two times, or three. The second price factor is adhesion. This refers to how well the new paint will stick to the walls (or ceilings). Some paints will tend to slide off if the walls aren't absolutely clean and free of grease. Others have the ability to stick to almost any surface, regardless of how grimy. The third factor is "spread"–how easily you can dip a brush or roller in and paint it on. Some paint is very thick, but simply won't spread well. Other paint seems thin, but spreads beautifully. To get good hide, adhesion, and spread, you generally need to buy the more expensive paints.

How much will brushes, drop cloths, and other equipment cost?   ☐ yes   ☐ no

You will undoubtedly need at least one if not two good brushes. Plan to spend $20 or more apiece for these.

Beyond the brushes, however, everything else is cheap. Rollers, dropcloths, wipes, blades, and so on can be easily bought at almost any building supply store. Of course, you'll also probably need ladders. When buying drop cloths, the tendency is to buy the cheapest plastic kind. However, the cost is based on how thick the plastic is and how big an area it will cover. The cheapest often are very thin, tear quickly, and easily get caught in ladders. Once again, spend a few bucks more to make your work far easier.

How much money will I save by doing it myself?   ☐ yes   ☐ no

As of this writing, the cost for painting the exterior of an average 2000-square-foot house (including trim) is about $1500 to 2500 depending on your area of the country. The cost for doing the inside is a bit less. Of course, prices will vary, as will the quality of painters. However, the cost of paint and materials for both inside and out could easily be under $1000. That means that you could save as much as $3500 or more by doing it yourself.

Is painting hard?   ☐ yes   ☐ no

It's hard work (although it doesn't usually require lifting anything heavier than paint cans), and it's dirty work. And then there are the odors. (Modern paints have reduced odors, which are supposed to be less toxic.) But most people can get into the knack of it very quickly. The hardest part is painting wood such as banisters, doors, and window trim. This requires the use of a brush and a smooth technique so as not to leave marks. A really good brush will make a world of difference. Be sure to ask people where you buy your paint and brushes about doing trim and woodwork. Often, someone can show you how in a matter of a few minutes. Of course, there are many books also available on the subject.

Should I use flat paint?   ☐ yes   ☐ no

Flat paint gives off a dull, flat finish. It is usually the choice for walls except in kitchens and baths. It is also frequently the choice for exteriors. The problem with flat paint is that it's very difficult to clean. Rubbing, as you might want to do if you get a stain, can quickly remove the paint. Many people prefer a "satin" finish, which is slightly more glossy and easier to keep clean.

Should I use glossy paint?   ☐ yes   ☐ no

A glossy paint has a bright, shiny surface. It's ideal for bathrooms and kitchens because very little sticks to it, and that which does can usually be wiped off. On the other hand, few people like to see a glossy, reflective surface on walls or ceilings of living areas (in the dining room, den, living room, or bedrooms). It's also frequently used on trim work, particularly on doorjambs and window trim. This is because these areas frequently get finger marks on them as people open and close doors and windows. The glossy paint makes the marks easier to remove.

What about stains?   ☐ yes   ☐ no

Paints obscure the surfaces that you are painting. Stains may also do this, or they may be transparent (or semi-transparent). Stains are typically used to treat woods. However, you don't need to use the same color stain as the type of wood. For example, you can get interesting effects by using oak stain on pine, or ash stain on mahogany. Generally speaking, if you are staining trim, you'll want to stain it *before* you apply it, and apply it after all other painting is finished. The reason is that you don't want to get paint from walls on the trim, nor stain from the trim on the walls. Once painted, the trim is usually applied with small finish nails that are countersunk, filled, and covered with a dab of stain.

Should I use latex paint?   ☐ yes   ☐ no

Latex-based paint has one huge advantage–it cleans up with soap and water. For this reason, it has become the overwhelming favorite of most amateur painters. However, it does have certain disadvantages. It doesn't spread nearly as well as oil-based paint, so it's more difficult to use on trim and doors. And its high-gloss versions are usually not as glossy as those of oil-based paints. Finally, it is more subject to mildew, so may not be the best choice in wet areas such as bathrooms. If you're painting over existing paint, match your paints. Paint latex over latex, and oil over oil.

Should I use oil-based paint?   ☐ yes   ☐ no

Oil- or alkyd-based paints must be thinned and cleaned with turpentine or paint thinner. It's smelly, there are some dangers to using the chemicals, and it's generally harder to apply than latex-based paint. However, for glossy surfaces, it usually gives a superior performance. Also, particularly when a fungicide is included, it's superior for bathrooms and kitchens. Generally speaking, oil-based paints must be brushed on. If you have a surface, such as cabinets, that already has oil-based paint on it, then use oil-based paints over it. Oil will tend to stick to oil.

What about removing old paint?   ☐ yes   ☐ no

Be careful. Old paint may contain lead. If it does, it should be removed by a professional. Do not try to remove lead paint by sanding, scraping, or burning. You'll only release the lead into the environment. Lead paint was banned after 1978, however, some existing stocks may have been used after that date. You can have your house tested for lead paint; however, it is costly. Check with *www.epa.gov* for tips on how to find a lead paint abatement service.

How do I get rid of old paint?   ☐ yes   ☐ no

If you find some old paint, you should probably not use it, since it might contain lead. Almost all paints must be disposed of at a toxic disposal site. Check with your local waste management service to find the one closest to you and the times available for drop-off.

Can I handle it if I get paint on carpets or furniture?   ☐ yes   ☐ no

No matter how many dropcloths you put down (indeed, putting down too many can be as much trouble as not enough!), no matter how careful you are, if you're painting an area that includes furniture (as is often the case when the renovated part of the house blends into the unchanged part), paint will inevitably get on something it isn't supposed to. If it gets on carpets or furniture, it spells big trouble, unless you're prepared to act quickly. With latex paint, having a dripping sponge and some clean, colorless rags ready for clean-up will make all the difference. Latex dries very quickly, and once dry, it's permanent. Thus, the key to removal is to get it off immediately after it drips on. Drowning the area with water will usually dilute the paint to the point where it can be absorbed by the rags. With oil-based paints, you have longer to get it off. However, paint thinner and turpentine can leave their own stains, which must then be removed.

Have I gotten at least three bids?   ☐ yes   ☐ no

If you've decided to have your home professionally painted, get at least three bids. You probably will be surprised at the spread between them. Remember, with painting it's mostly labor. And the bid can vary depending on how hungry for the job the painter is. Don't assume that the highest bid means the best job or the lowest means the worst. Get references and check them out. See some previous work the painter did, and ask the owners how satisfied they were. Did the painter avoid getting paint on anything? Did he or she promptly clean up? Did he or she use good paint? Don't make your decision based just on price.

Questions to Ask the Painter

Are you licensed?   ☐ yes   ☐ no

Some painters are, and some are not. Quite frankly, it's not like being a plumber or an electrician. While being licensed as a contractor has some benefits (mostly to the painter—it allows him or her to sue you more easily if you don't pay!), it doesn't mean the unlicensed person will necessarily do a bad job. If it were a large job, for example, the whole house, I'd probably want to be dealing with a licensed painter. On the other hand, if it's just a room, a handyman might do just as well, and be a bit cheaper.

Can you give me nearby references?   ☐ yes   ☐ no

This, of course, is crucial. Many painters will show you pictures of homes they've painted. That's not good enough. You need to know the location of the homes and the names of the owners. For an exterior, you can just drive by. But for an interior, it's different. You need to call the owner and ask if you can come by and take a look. Most owners are very glad to have you come by. They enjoy showing off the good work, or complaining about the job if it was a bad one. Don't forget to ask how clean the painter was, whether paint got on any carpeting or furnishings, and how the final cleanup went.

When can you start?   ☐ yes   ☐ no

Getting a start date is very important, if you're working on a time schedule. It's no good to wait until all the renovation work is done and then look for a good painter. The good ones are tied up for weeks, sometimes months in advance. Find the painter early, decide when your other work will be finished, and then get a start date. It's a lot easier for you to call the painter and get a postponement of a week or so, than it is to call up and say you need the job done right now.

Will you continue until finished?   ☐ yes   ☐ no

Ideally, you want to be dealing directly with the painter himself or herself. You want the painter to tell you that he or she won't start your job until whatever else he or she is painting is finished. If you're just dealing with a salesperson for a painting firm, they might have half a dozen jobs in the works. If they all "gel" at the same time, a crew could come out, start working on your home, then leave not to return for a week or more. You want a commitment, hopefully put in writing, that once started on your job, the painter will continue until it's completed.

Can I be in the house while you're working?   ☐ yes   ☐ no

Chances are you're not doing a whole-house renovation. If that's the case, you probably don't want the extra expense of staying at a nearby motel while the painting is done. Ask the painter if he or she can mask and seal off the part of the home you're living in while the painting goes on. No, it won't be peaches and cream because you'll still have the paint smells, particularly if oil-based paints are used. But at least you'll be able to avoid moving out.

Will you guarantee protection of all furniture, carpets, and so on?

☐ yes   ☐ no

Get the guarantee in writing. The painter probably won't be working in the area of the house where you're living (and have carpets and furniture). However, there's the blending of the old with the new, and at the juncture, there's great opportunity for paint spills to get on expensive items. Be sure that the painter guarantees not to get paint on any of your valued things. Most painters will give you this guarantee. They take great pride in their work, and part of the job is cleanliness. If a painter won't guarantee to avoid getting paint slopped on your things, you might want to consider using a different painter.

Will you give me a bid for labor alone?

☐ yes   ☐ no

The problem with getting a job bid from a painter is that he or she may give you a low bid and make up for it by buying cheaper paint. The difference between the cost of good and mediocre paint can be as much as $500 or more, and that's money that can go right into the pocket of the painter. Besides, most painters know that the average person can't tell, when paint's been freshly applied, if it's good paint or cheap. If you get a labor-only price from the painter, then you can add to that the cost of the paint to ensure that only the best-quality paint is purchased.

Can I buy my own paint?

☐ yes   ☐ no

One way to get the best paint is to buy it yourself. Some painters will go along with this, but few will like it. Most painters have a preferred paint because they are used to working with it, they know how well it applies, and how much it takes. You may want to use a different brand of paint, and they may be unfamiliar with it and hesitant to use it. Besides, if you buy the paint, you won't get the painter's discount at the paint store. Perhaps a better way to go is to specify the brand, type, and color of paint to be used and let the painter buy it.

How long will the smell last?   ☐ yes   ☐ no

It won't hurt to ask. With oil-based paints, expect the odor to remain strong for a week or more. With latex-based paints, expect it to last for at least a day or so. Your painter, however, may have had other experiences, may be using special paints, or may have made allowances for clearing the air out of the area being painted. Be sure to ask.

14
Demolition and Cleanup

Questions to Ask Yourself

Will I handle the demolition?

☐ yes   ☐ no

Many owners feel that demolition is an area where they can do the work themselves and save some money. The reasoning goes, "How can I mess up? After all, it's demolition!" You can do it. However, you should be aware that there are many hidden problems with demolition. First, there's the matter of demolishing only as much as is necessary. Sometimes you don't know how much to take out, until you've started. You don't want to take out good material that should be saved. Second, there's the matter of doing it. Demolition can be hard, backbreaking work involving a sledgehammer, and then a heavy wheelbarrow to haul out the debris. Most average people just aren't up to it. Finally, there's the safety issue. Sometimes the materials you are dealing with will be toxic (lead, asbestos, black mold), and could injure you. Also, very often, people who do demolition work get injured, from minor cuts and scrapes to more serious injuries. And there's always the chance of cutting through a live electrical wire or water pipe. (Be sure that *all power is off* before doing any demolition work.) Do you really want to take the risk yourself? Wouldn't it be easier and safer to call in a professional?

Have I rented a dumpster?

☐ yes   ☐ no

Demolished materials must be hauled somewhere. The easiest way to handle them is to get rid of them right from the start—no moving the stuff twice. That usually means renting a dumpster into which the materials can be dumped. Be aware, however, that regardless of how large dumpsters (or smaller "Clementinas") look, they all have maximum-weight limitations. If you're hauling concrete and tile, a dumpster with 6-foot sides may only be capable of hauling 12 inches of debris. Check with the rental agency. (Dumpster rentals are listed in the yellow pages.) Also, be aware that your home may contain toxic materials from lead to asbestos and these must NOT be thrown out with the other debris. Rather, they have to be disposed of at a toxic waste dump site.

Am I in accordance with building code and HOA work rules?

☐ yes   ☐ no

Demolishing old parts of a house is often a very loud and dusty job. Typically, the local building code will demand that it only be done between certain hours, say 8:00 in the morning and 10:00 in the evening. Local Home Owner's Association rules may be even more stringent only allowing a small window of time, say from 9:00 in the morning to 4:00 in the afternoon. Be sure that you check what the regulations are in your area. Violations can bring stiff fines, not to mention angry neighbors.

Will I need to clean up each day?

☐ yes   ☐ no

Many people feel that if they're doing the demolition, they don't have to follow the rules. (They feel that rules are only for contractors!) Many cities and HOAs require you to clean up around the property after each workday. That includes the street in front as well as around the house. Safety dictates that you also clean up the floor inside the house.

Am I prepared to seal off livable areas of the house?

☐ yes   ☐ no

Be prepared to do this *before* you begin. Heavy plastic sheeting (1 mil. or thicker) can often be used to separate the living from the working area. Be sure that you use duct tape or other heavy-duty material to hold the plastic down. Even a small hole can allow sometimes toxic dust and debris to migrate from one area of the house to another. It's almost impossible to control noise (unless you can isolate one area of the house behind walls and doors), so most people simply don't even bother to try.

Will I be able to live with the mess and inconvenience? ☐ yes ☐ no

You may be without a kitchen. (You might create a temporary kitchen in the garage.) Perhaps you'll be down to one bath only. (You can't inhabit a house without a bathroom.) Every time people go from the work area to the living area, they may track sawdust, dirt, and even oils around. This means the floors will need to be covered in plastic, or they could get stained. If you're the sort of person who is easily adaptable, you probably can live through any mess. However, many homeowners find the mess impossible and after a time simply move out to a temporary apartment or motel.

Will I be able to live with the noise? ☐ yes ☐ no

Even if you can handle the mess and the inconvenience, the noise can be deafening. An electric rotary handsaw can produce over 90 decibels of noise, up close, almost as loud as a jet engine heard from a distance. Electric drills, chisels, and other devices are also quite loud. And there's nothing you can do about this, since these tools are necessary to getting the job done. One thing you may be able to control is the boom box music that many workers seem to enjoy. You can ban it from the job site. However, in turn, you risk the anger of the workers.

Have I identified materials that I want to save? ☐ yes ☐ no

Your home may have an old banister or even old stairs that are worth saving. If you don't want to put them into the renovation, you may want to use them again somewhere else . . . or sell them. Your home may have stained glass windows or even just oak plank floorboards that you want to hang onto. Before you start demolition, it's important to go through your house and inventory the items to be saved. If you're not sure, you may want to invite an expert along, even if you need to pay that expert. Don't rely just on the contractor's opinion of what to save, as he or she may have little experience with antiques and with old accouterments.

Do I have a place to save materials that are removed?   ☐ yes   ☐ no

Designate a certain area that will be used to store materials you've saved. This should be an area that doesn't contain new supplies, lest the two be confused. It should also be an area that doesn't have a lot of traffic, lest somebody bang into your stained glass window or banister and scratch or break it. A garage or portion of a garage may be useful. Try an attic or basement, if the area's not involved in the renovation. As a last resort, you may want to ask a neighbor to use a portion of his or her garage or even rent a space at a rental unit yard.

How do I remove ceramic tile?   ☐ yes   ☐ no

The only question is, do you want to try and save the tile? Saving tile is very difficult, particularly if it was well laid and adhered to the mortar. Besides breaking it out without chipping the edges, you must also chip away the mortar on the back without breaking the tile. In my experience, you'll be lucky to save one out of three or four tiles. If saving the tile is not an issue, then the usual way of removing tile is to smash it with a sledge hammer, break it into smaller pieces, and haul it off to the dumpster. Keep in mind that when you get tile and mortar, you create very heavy, sharp, dangerous pieces, sometimes weighing 50 pounds or more. Don't do this if you have back or other problems limiting your ability to lift heavy weights.

How do I remove old paint?   ☐ yes   ☐ no

This is very tricky. If the paint was produced prior to 1978, it may have lead in it. If so, then only a lead mitigation company should remove it. If the paint was produced after 1978, it probably does not contain lead (some old stocks of paint were still used after this date). In this case, several methods will work, such as sanding or using chemicals. Burning the paint with a torch will remove it, but is not recommended because it can release toxic smoke into the air, much of which you may breathe.

How do I remove wallboard?

yes ☐ no ☐

Wallboard is typically nailed every six inches onto studs. The only problem with removing it is that you may leave the nails, which then have to be removed one at a time (if you're going to save the studs). You really don't need a sledgehammer for wall board—the sledge is too heavy and the board too fragile. A simple hammer to knock holes in it and then using a crowbar to peel it back usually works. Be careful when doing ceilings, as they have a tendency to fall in clumps, onto your head if you're not quickly moving out of the way.

How do I remove old wood?

yes ☐ no ☐

Try using a "cuts all." This is a device with a reciprocating blade at one end that, as the name implies, will cut almost anything (including your hand, if you're not very careful!). It will cut old wood, nails, and plaster—almost anything depending on the blade used. These cost around $100. They can be used to cut out pieces of wood making them easier to remove. Don't try disassembling the old wood in the reverse order of how it was nailed together. This takes a long time and is rarely successful. Be careful of removing supporting studs and beams—you don't want a ceiling falling on you! And watch out for nails sticking out of wood—stepping on them can be nasty and require a quick trip to the hospital for a tetanus shot and other treatment.

What if black mold is discovered?

yes ☐ no ☐

This is liable to be found in any wet area. As of this writing, black mold has not been labeled as causing serious disease by the CDC (Center for Disease Control). However, some people are allergic to its spores, and some believe that it can cause serious illness. Use caution. You may want to wear protective gear as well as a protective breathing apparatus. You may want to call in a service that specializes in its removal. Removal may require different methods depending on how serious an infestation is involved. For very serious black mold, cutting out the boards and materials it is on may be the only solution. For minor infestations, I've found that a weak chlorine bleach solution may be helpful. If you're not sure, contact a termite/pest exterminator for help.

What if asbestos is uncovered?   ☐ yes   ☐ no

Asbestos is an excellent insulator. It is frequently found wrapped around heating ducts and other pipes. It may be found in floor tiles. And it has many other uses. When it's exposed, there are two remedies that are commonly used. One is encapsulation so that the fibers cannot come loose and escape into the environment. The other is to have it professionally removed. You should not attempt removal yourself, as you might make the situation worse. For example, vacuuming asbestos dust usually only spreads it out, as the fibers are too small to be captured by most vacuum cleaner bags. Check *www.epa.gov* for the name and location of the nearest asbestos mitigation service.

What if lead paint is discovered?   ☐ yes   ☐ no

Lead paint is considered toxic. It should be professionally removed and disposed of at a toxic waste site. Do not attempt to burn lead paint off wood, as you'll just introduce toxic lead smoke into the air. Do not attempt to vacuum the dust, as most vacuum cleaner bags are not capable of containing it. Do not attempt to sand wood that is covered with lead paint, as you will introduce lead into the air and onto the floor. Be sure not to burn wood covered with lead paint, outside, in fireplaces, or anywhere else. It just releases the lead into the air as part of the smoke. Check with a lead mitigation service near you by looking up *www.epa.gov*.

What if there's decayed wood?   ☐ yes   ☐ no

All rotten and decayed wood should be removed, as it will have lost its structural strength. Dry rot (which occurs in moist areas) may turn wood into mush. Beetles, termites, and ants can bore holes into it to the point where it will break away like dust. Sometimes coating the replacement wood with copper sulfate (a green, paintlike material) will prevent the new wood from rotting as well.

What if electrical wires are cut?
☐ yes   ☐ no

Chances are when your home was built an electrician ran wiring all through the walls (which were then exposed) in whatever manner was most convenient for him or her. Now, when you're demolishing walls, you may come across this wiring. As part of the demolition process, you may need to reposition this wiring to other locations. Be sure you do this in accordance with the local building code. The real danger, however, is that while demolishing a wall or ceiling, you'll accidentally cut through a wire. For that reason, all power to the house should be off when doing demolition. Cutting through a live electric wire can produce a severe shock. *Be sure all power to the house is off before and during any demolition work.*

What if plumbing lines need to be moved?
☐ yes   ☐ no

Try not to smash any plumbing lines when doing demolition. You may eventually need to move them, but in the meantime, try to leave them in place. This will help you determine what they are used for and where they go. This is particularly the case with vents. When moving plumbing lines, be sure that the new lines are in conformity with your local building code. It sometimes requires great creativity to move plumbing lines when you take out a wall, since the space they occupied is no longer available. Check with a good plumber for suggestions.

Am I prepared for health and safety issues?
☐ yes   ☐ no

Whether you or someone else handles demolition, it's always going to be a dangerous job. There's the dust that can be inhaled; the flying bits of tile, cement, and rock; and the wallboard that can fall on you. There are also environmental hazards such as lead, asbestos, formaldehyde, black mold, and others that are used in building materials and to which the person handling demolition will get exposed. Finally, there's the weight. Just carrying out the various items that have been knocked down can take a very strong person. Are you ready for this? Wouldn't it make more sense to hire a professional to do it?

Can I handle injuries of others?   ☐ yes   ☐ no

On almost all renovations of any size, someone will get hurt during the demolition or construction. The injuries are usually very minor, but they can also be life threatening. Renovation work is simply dangerous. It's a good idea to know in advance how to transport someone quickly to a hospital and which nearby hospital has a good emergency room available. Also be sure that everyone working on the job is covered by health insurance and workman's compensation.

Am I prepared for a fire hazard?   ☐ yes   ☐ no

We almost never think of this during renovation, but each year a goodly number of homes burn down during the process. There are many reasons. Broken electrical wiring can produce shorts, which can lead to a fire. A plumber soldering copper pipe uses a torch, which if not used carefully, can easily start a fire. Many operations, from preparing tar to heating linoleum, use flame and have the potential to start fires. Be sure that you have fire extinguishers, fully charged, handy throughout the job site. Be sure everyone knows where they are. And check with your homeowner's insurance to be sure that it's effective during renovation and that your property is fully covered.

Have I rented a portable toilet?   ☐ yes   ☐ no

Many building departments insist that a toilet be made available whenever workmen are on the job. If you can demonstrate that one of your house toilets is always available and operating, that will probably suffice. Otherwise, you may need to rent a portable toilet. These are readily available from rental stores, but they often cost several hundred dollars. It's usually an added expense that's rarely budgeted for. The portable toilets will almost certainly be needed from demolition through cleanup.

Have I set up a temporary kitchen?   ☐ yes   ☐ no

Although it probably doesn't meet building code standards, many homeowners who are having their kitchens renovated, yet continue to live in their homes, set up a temporary kitchen in extra bathrooms or sometimes in garages. If you do, be sure that you've got a sanitary counter and that there's no chance of mixing potable water with wastewater. Sometimes, particularly during good weather, it's possible to set up your kitchen outside on the patio using your barbecue for cooking. Making a camping adventure out of it can turn a problem into a fun experience for the entire family.

Have I alerted my neighbors? ☐ yes ☐ no

None of us lives in a vacuum, and our neighbors are going to be impacted by any renovation we do. There will be the construction noise, the trucks rumbling up and down the street, and the dust and dirt. And there are always the extra problems, like a water pipe that bursts and floods a neighbor's yard. As a result, it's usually a good idea to prepare your neighbors. *After* you've obtained all your permissions from the building department, planning commission, and homeowner's association (so your neighbors can't petition to have you stop the work), let them know what you're planning on doing, how big the scope of the work is, and how long it will take. You may even want to bring over a present to let them know that you care about their feelings. Be sure that you leave a phone number where they can contact you at any time. Often, neighbors can spot a problem (such as a fire) before you have any idea of its existence.

Have I called for demolition and cleanup inspections? ☐ yes ☐ no

Many building departments demand that you allow them to inspect the property *after* all demolition work is completed, but *before* you start any new construction. Some homeowner's associations will want to inspect your property on a weekly, sometimes daily, basis to be sure that you're keeping the work area clean. Be sure to comply with all inspection demands, or else you might be shut down, or worse, be required to rip out work that's been completed.

Questions to Ask Your Contractor

Will you handle all demolition? ☐ yes ☐ no

If you're working with a remodeling contractor, the answer almost certainly will be yes. The remodeling contractor wants to handle demolition so he or she can be sure to take out enough of the old to put in the new, but not so much that work is wasted. If you have a general contractor who's new to renovation, he or she may instead be planning simply to hire a couple of laborers to come in and do the demolition. If the latter is the case, you may want to be on side during the work to supervise and see that the job is done right.

Will you agree to clean up each day after work? ☐ yes ☐ no

This should be in your contract with penalties for failure to comply. This is especially the case if your home owner's association or building department has strict cleanup rules. Remember, they won't go after the contractor; they'll go after you. And the only way you can force the contractor to comply is if you have a cleanup clause in the contract. Don't be caught short because some agency is demanding that you do cleanup work while you don't have the power to enforce it on your contractor.

Will you agree to clean up after the job is complete? ☐ yes ☐ no

This should go without saying. However, some contractors need to be nudged. Be sure you have a rock-solid agreement that after the job is completed, the contractor will police the grounds and remove any and all remaining building supplies, remnants from the demolition, tools (broken as well as good), and anything else brought onto the job site. The contractor should leave the interior clean and swept. The exterior should be clean and ready for landscaping. (Typically, you will hire a separate contractor to handle your landscaping, unless you do it yourself.)

Will you agree to limit noise? ☐ yes ☐ no

Most contractors are very hesitant to agree to this since it's so subjective. What one person considers objectionable noise, another may find merely annoying. Usually contractors will agree to do their best to keep noise down, but not agree to a silent job. After all, they need to use power tools to get their work done. Be sure, however, that they agree in writing to limit or eliminate any radios, CDs, or other loud music. Sometimes workers play music very loudly, and it can annoy not only you, but can also make your neighbors angry.

Will you seal off the area being worked on from the rest of the house?   ☐ yes   ☐ no

Typically, the best you'll get here is a promise to try. Any honest contractor will point out that he or she will use plastic or cloth or in some cases temporary walls to isolate your living area from the work area. But in spite of the best of intentions, dust and dirt will inevitably migrate to your part of the home. To suggest anything else is simply not being forthright. However, the contractor should indicate that he or she will do their level best to keep the dirt and dust down to a minimum. There's really very little else you can demand.

Will you properly handle all toxic materials?   ☐ yes   ☐ no

All good contractors will. But some less scrupulous contractors may simply deal with toxic materials the same as with normal materials. This can not only be hazardous to their health, but to yours as well. You want a contractor who can recognize toxic materials and deal with them appropriately.

15
Adding a Deck

Questions to Ask Yourself

Is my old deck in bad condition?

☐ **yes** ☐ **no**

It's usually far easier to renovate an existing deck that's in good condition than to put in a new one. Renovation includes fixing nails and screws that have popped, replacing rotted wood, and then painting or staining. Care must be exercised to see that the existing deck is structurally sound. Sometimes dry rot will get into the support timbers, particularly if they are in a wet location, weakening them. It may simply be easier to replace a rotted deck with totally new materials than to save it.

Where should I put a new deck?

☐ **yes** ☐ **no**

The location of a new deck is important not only for convenience, but also to the appearance of your home. Rear decks are easier to place since their appearance is not as critical to the home's overall look. Front decks must be in conformity with the overall style of the home and should not overshadow the entrance. Be sure to consider how you will achieve access to the deck. For example, if you're going to use it to barbecue, be sure it's near your kitchen. If children will be playing on it, you will want to be able to see it easily from inside the house so you can keep an eye on them.

How big should I make the deck?

☐ **yes** ☐ **no**

For most people the rule is simply, "The bigger, the better." Not necessarily. Size should depend on use. If it's going to be a walkway, then it only really needs to be about 4 feet wide. A patio deck can easily be only 10 feet by 10 feet. Add a few more feet for a barbecue. Remember, deck space you never use is wasted. And these days, decks are very expensive.

Do I need a set of plans?   ☐ yes   ☐ no

Unless your deck is going to sit right on the ground (or not more than about a foot above it), you will need a set of plans. These needn't be full-scale blueprints, but they should be detailed enough so that a contractor or building inspector can tell the kind of wood you're using, the various sizes, the depth and width of footings, the metal connectors you'll use, and so forth.

Do I need a permit?   ☐ yes   ☐ no

If your deck involves any sort of construction and is off the ground, then you almost certainly will need a permit. However, don't worry. Most building departments have special permits for homeowner decks. They may even have a set of standard plans that you can adapt to your usage. There will, however, be a fee for a plan check and for inspections. It might be nominal, just $35. Or it could be several hundreds of dollars, depending on how reliant on building department revenues your city is. Usually, you can apply for and get your permit in a single visit to the building department, *if* you have a set of plans available.

Should I use real wood?   ☐ yes   ☐ no

Almost certainly you'll use wood for the beams and posts that make up the support system of the deck. However, for the decking material itself, natural woods are very expensive. The most commonly used woods are redwood, cedar, and other woods that resist weathering and rot.

Should I use synthetics?   ☐ yes   ☐ no

Synthetic planks that can be used as decking are now available in a variety of compositions varying from fiberglass to pressed wood fibers to salvaged tires and bottles. In years past, they were usually considered too expensive to use, but today they are competitive with most wood decking. Their disadvantage is that they usually don't look quite as good as wood. On the other hand, they typically stand up better to weather, never need painting or staining, and when screwed into place, rarely come loose.

Should I use treated (green) wood?   ☐ yes   ☐ no

Pressure-treated wood, also called "green" wood because of its color, is sometimes recommended for decks because it contains a fungicide that keeps the boards from rotting. However, be aware that it may contain arsenic or other harmful ingredients. Therefore, its use is increasingly banned by building departments. You certainly wouldn't want to use pressure-treated wood as decking where someone might pick up a sliver. And care must be taken when sawing the wood not to inhale dust particles. Additionally, the wood may not be burned, as the smoke can be toxic.

What color should my deck be?   ☐ yes   ☐ no

The color should complement the color of the house as well as the grain of the wood. However, cross staining is often very attractive. That's when you use a different color stain than the wood, for example, redwood stain on pine. If you paint the deck, be sure that it's not going to clash with the house color.

Will I put a cover over my deck?   ☐ yes   ☐ no

Decks are great for sunning. However, if the sun is hot, you'll need a cover. Permanent deck covers require building permits, plans, and sturdy construction. For this reason, many people opt for an umbrella as an inexpensive, effective sunshade.

Should I build the deck myself?   ☐ yes   ☐ no

This is probably the most commonly tackled renovation project by homeowners, more so by far than kitchens, baths, or bedrooms. It not only seems easier, but actually is easier than most others. However, be sure you spend some time familiarizing yourself with deck construction.

You'll need to know about ledgers (faceplates that connect the deck to the house), footings (cement piers that anchor the deck to the ground), joist hangers (metal connectors that hold the beams in place), and a host of other building materials. Check into one of the many books on deck design available at bookstores or building supply houses. And always be prepared for the heavy lifting and dangers of construction work.

Should I remove the old deck myself?   ☐ yes   ☐ no

You can. Be be aware that there may be black mold, dry rot, termites and other infestation in it which may require special handling and disposal. In addition there's the weight of the materials as well as the danger from falling boards, protruding nails, and demolition in general.

Have I compared materials prices?   ☐ yes   ☐ no

Check with a building supply company for a deck package. Usually, you can come in with your plans, and if they are detailed enough (showing how much lumber you need and what sizes, what metal connectors, how much cement, screws, nails, and so on), the store will put together an invoice for all of the materials, tack on a discount because you're buying it all at once, and in some locations, deliver it right to your house! But still compare prices between different suppliers. You probably will find them fairly close, since materials costs don't vary that much. But you may be able to save a few bucks by going to a cheaper supplier.

Will I put in the footings and piers?   ☐ yes   ☐ no

You may have every intention of building the deck yourself. However, you may also find it wiser to have professionals sink the footings. Depending on your climate, you may need to dig holes as much as 2 feet deep and wide, fill them with concrete (including supporting rebars), and use metal post holders. This is not brain surgery, but it is heavy work. And getting the concrete where you want it in back of your home can be tricky. It's so much easier simply to begin building with wood on top of a professionally prepared foundation than it is to start from scratch.

What about using diagonal bracing?

☐ yes   ☐ no

Few decks collapse from weight pushing directly down (provided that they were engineered properly). Most fail because of side pressure from wind, earthquakes, or even a leaning house. The way to prevent this is to use adequate diagonal bracing. These are wood or metal boards attached to the piers that support the deck. They create triangles of strength. And as everyone knows, a triangle (unlike a square or rectangle) cannot be bent. The more diagonal bracing you use, the stronger your deck will be.

Should I use metal connectors?

☐ yes   ☐ no

Metal connectors include such things as post holders, T-braces, spacers, and other pieces of metal that are used to connect the wood of the deck. Years ago, connectors were frequently made of wood, which unfortunately can dry out and crack, or get wet and rot. Today, although not always required by building departments, metal connectors (made of steel and sometimes coated to prevent rusting) are your best bet. They are stronger and more permanent.

Should I use a sealer?

☐ yes   ☐ no

Natural wood should be sealed. Behr, Olympic, and other brands also make stains that seal the deck and can make it more attractive. It is important to seal the deck as soon as it is constructed to prevent the wood from drying out and cracking. Once the wood begins to deteriorate, it cannot be rejuvenated. Adding stain belatedly will prevent further damage, but will not alleviate damage already done.

Questions to Ask Your Contractor

Do you have a standard set of deck plans?

☐ yes   ☐ no

Many contractors do. They have a standard set that they can then usually modify to fit your needs. Using their plans can avoid the cost of having plans drawn up. Additionally, the contractor probably has built this deck before, hence knows how much the materials and labor will cost, and can give you a highly accurate bid.

Do I need an architect?   ☐ **yes**   ☐ **no**

If your contractor does not have a standard set, he or she may insist that you provide plans. If you can't draw them yourself, you'll need to get an architect to do them for you. This is usually quite expensive. Alternatively, you can often find deck plans in magazines specializing in the field. Often, for under $500, you can write off for a complete set of plans that can be adapted to your use.

Will you get a permit?   ☐ **yes**   ☐ **no**

If you need a permit to build a deck, your contractor needs one as well. However, some contractors don't want to take the time and bother with the hassle of inspections (and corrective work that inspectors may require). Hence, they may say that no permit is needed and plan on just doing the job without one. The problem here is that if you ever sell your home, you'll need to disclose that the deck was built without benefit of permit. And that could squelch a sale or undercut your price. It's better to insist on the contractor's getting the needed permit, even if you have to be the one to run down to the building department to get it.

Can you give me an accurate bid?   ☐ **yes**   ☐ **no**

Unlike with renovation work where it's difficult to price until the existing parts of the house are removed, a deck is usually easy to bid. Even if an old deck needs to be removed, it's usually possible to see the ground and get a solid idea of the work involved. Therefore, expect a highly accurate bid. Be wary if the contractor says he or she can't tell for sure and wants to give you a time and materials bid. This might just be a way to force the price up.

How long will it take?   ☐ **yes**   ☐ **no**

As with pricing, it should be easy for the contractor to take a look and determine just how long it will take. Keep in mind that building a deck usually requires setting cement footings. It can take a few days to dig the holes and prepare the steel reinforcement bars, a day to pour, and a week or more for the cement to properly dry and harden. Therefore, even though the contractor may be able to put the beams and planks together in two or three days, don't expect the deck itself to be completed in anything less than several weeks.

Index

About the Author

Robert Irwin, one of America's leading experts in all areas of real estate, is the author of more than 40 books, including McGraw-Hill's best-selling Tips and Traps series and *Home Buyer's Checklist*. For more real estate tips and traps, go to www.robertirwin.com